A PEACE

Unfettered

MY ANTHOLOGY OF FAITH

QENÉ MANON JEFFERS

WESTBOW
PRESS®
A DIVISION OF THOMAS NELSON
& ZONDERVAN

WestBow Press books may be ordered through booksellers or by contacting:

WestBow Press
A Division of Thomas Nelson & Zondervan
1663 Liberty Drive
Bloomington, IN 47403
www.westbowpress.com
1 (866) 928-1240

ISBN: 978-1-9736-1208-7 (sc)
ISBN: 978-1-9736-1207-0 (hc)
ISBN: 978-1-9736-1209-4 (e)

Library of Congress Control Number: 2017919540

Print information available on the last page.

WestBow Press rev. date: 02/13/2018

Contents

Letters from My Family and Friends

—⟶⟞⟝⟞—

I was playing sandlot baseball with a bunch of guys from the neighborhood when I first saw her ride up on her bike with her best friend. But at that moment I wasn't thinking about marriage or children. I had no idea that one day I would marry this girl and that God would call us both at the same time—her to salvation and me to preach the gospel. I didn't think that we would have three children and ten grandchildren; I was thinking about the baseball game that the guys and I were playing. I was fifteen, and she was twelve, and even though I wasn't even thinking about marriage, there was just something about her that I couldn't get out of my mind.

I know now that it was God showing me that He had chosen this one for me. I still carry her sixth grade picture in my wallet—if you ask me, I will show it to you! It's hard to believe that it has been over fifty years since the day that I first met Qené. Since that day, with God's help, we have built a wonderful life together. Like the binding on a beautiful book, our lives and the experiences that we have shared have brought us closer together and have served to prepare us for the assignment that God has called us to.

But these are not just our experiences; every one of you can relate to these stories and can apply the principles of them to your own life and your own experience. God has gifted Qené in such a way that these life experiences have become like highlighted chapters that we may return to over and over to find comfort and peace.

The apostle Paul wrote, "You are our epistle written in our hearts, known and read of all men" (2 Corinthians 3:2 NKJV).

All of us have a story to tell. The stories in this book tell about a life miraculously changed by the grace, love, and longsuffering of the Lord. If you are in Christ, this is your story too. A story that is "known and read by all men." My prayer is that this book may be a source of blessing to all who pick it up and pour over its pages.

I am so very thankful that God chose this one for me. I love her with an everlasting love.

—Pat Jeffers Sr., Q.'s husband and pastor

March 17, 2016, was possibly the scariest day of my life. That day, I sat in the emergency room and then in ICU with my dad as we watched my mom struggle for every breath she took. She had been sick for almost a week, and before we knew it, she had taken a turn for the worse. We had no idea what trials the next few weeks would bring for her and us as she fought for her life. Pastors came to pray. Friends gathered to offer a hug and a word of encouragement. Doctors worked around the clock to find a treatment that would spare her life.

During those *long* days in the hospital, I would search through my mom's story files on her Facebook account to find words of encouragement and stories that would make us smile. Even while she was lying in a hospital bed on a ventilator near death, she was bringing us hope and encouragement through her stories.

The Lord allowed my mom to overcome that illness. He gave her breath for another day.

I pray that Mom's stories encourage you and uplift your spirit. Maybe her life was spared especially for you, the reader of this book. My prayer is that you receive a special touch from the Lord as you read and that each story will minister to you whether you're in the middle of a trial or standing high on a mountaintop. With every story, I pray that your faith will become bigger than your fear.

—Jené Barker, Q.'s daughter

I've known Qené for almost twenty-five years. For the first few I knew her as my pastor's wife. And now, for nearly twenty years, she has been my mother-in-law and NéNé to my children. My first memory of Qené, however, is a spiritual lesson she shared at a camp. I was in the third grade, and the lesson she taught was about buttoning your shirt. Yes, it truly was a spiritual lesson, and it has stuck with me after all these years.

There are many things I love about Qené, but one of my favorites is listening to her stories. For as long as I have known her, she has never failed to entertain me with a new story about her life, ranging from her childhood to an incident that may have just happened the day before. Most of the time these stories have everyone in the room in stitches, especially her children and grandchildren. And just when I think I've heard them all, she surprises me with a new tale. I can't count the number of times I've said, "How have I never heard this story before?"

There's always something great to hear from Qené, and as is her gift, she can turn any of her tales into a lesson for those listening that helps them draw closer to Jesus or to find hope or comfort in their situations. I hope this book speaks to you in the way Qené's stories have spoken to me over all these years.

—Brandon Barker, Q.'s son-in-law

When driving to see Mom each day during those long weeks in the hospital, Linsey and Sadi and I described our weariness like it was a fog over our day. But quickly after we'd go in to see Mom, I felt a wash of renewed spirit and energy! Mom has had that effect on a lot of people over the years.

Her years of serving the public at Division of Family Services and in ministry with Dad have allowed her to touch many lives. Mom's kindness and total care for people has always captured me. She impacts people with her spirit of service and kindness.

After all these years of being her firstborn, my mother still teaches me and shows me how to treat others. Even in sickness she remains concerned about others around her. Even in tough times when we didn't have two pennies to rub together, I remember she always found a way to share with others. It's because she follows Christ. And she doesn't just walk with Him; she chases Him like a child chases after a parent.

Lord, I ask today that you would use our family to bless others. Even in our time of distress, You gave us opportunity to minister to others who were hurting and in need of You. Please use Mom's book to do the same. Amen.

—P. J. and Sadi Jeffers, Q.'s son and daughter-in-law

I have had the pleasure of working with Qené Jeffers for several years now, and I refer to her as "my" Q. We immediately clicked as though we had known each other forever. There is no other woman on the face of this earth that I would trust wholeheartedly as much as this woman. She is an incredible woman of God with a quirky, fun mannerism. You can't help but love her! She genuinely loves people and is such an encourager to others.

Qené loves to share her life stories, inviting you to go down memory lane with her. I find myself so intrigued when she begins to tell a story—I never know if I will end up laughing or crying, but you can bet if it is a Q. story, it is going to be worth listening to. I hope you enjoy reading this book and becoming intrigued as much as I have. From her childhood stories to her conversion to her love story with her sweet Pat to her miraculous healing, she tells her life stories with so much passion, detail, and yes, sometimes lots of humor.

Oh, and did I tell you how much of a prayer warrior this woman is? Ask her to pray for anything, and she is on it with diligence. She knows her scriptures well and regularly refers to God's Word and His promises. Have a need or a concern? Ask Q. to pray, and you got it! Have a fear? Have a health issue? Can't sleep? Yes, even if you want snow. Ask Q. to pray! There is nothing too big or small that Qené will not go to the throne of God for you. How comforting to know that at a moment's notice, you can call on someone and she is there for you! When this woman was in the hospital literally on her death bed, she sent me a text around 2:00 a.m. wanting to know how *I* was feeling. She had heard that I had been sick. Really? Who does that? Q. does that! She is genuinely concerned for others—so much so that even on her death bed she is reaching for her phone to call a friend to check on her.

If you want to know more about this incredible woman and her faith and her passion for life, I encourage you to read this book as my Q. shares her stories with you. You will be absolutely amazed at her testimony of talking with and seeing Jesus as she lay in the hospital wondering if life on this earth was going to end for her. Her vivid descriptions will leave you in awe. I pray this leaves you as inspired and encouraged as it has me. What faith! What victory! What a peace unfettered!

—Torrie Thompson, personal friend and sister in Christ

When my children were young and we were surviving on one modest income, I was always looking for ways to economize. A family friend had just bought us our first computer, and I thought, *Why not use it as a cookbook?* Low and behold, as I did a search for "hot chocolate mix," I found myself at a pastors' wives forum. I didn't know such things even existed!

I stayed and began to interact with these dear sisters. I found a wonderful community there, and it was such a blessing in my life. In the years that followed, I found sweet fellowship and a place of belonging in this online community. I had a common ground with women of kindred spirit as we struggled under the load of the enormous job of being married to ministry.

One of the lovely women I met there had a very odd name: "Qené." It was unusual, and pretty and unique, and a very special name indeed. And as I began to get to know this Qené, I found that she herself was just as unique and lovely as her name.

I have never heard or read anything negative from her. She always speaks with love, and the grace and compassion of God just pours from her. I found her self-proclaimed quirkiness charming, and it was, and still is, a delight to know her.

Qené is very good at loving. When one of the younger pastors' wives was not acting very Christ-like, she responded by loving her anyway. When one of us was hurting, she was compassionate and kind—always kind. When she disagreed strongly with one of us, she was not afraid to say so—yet even then we knew and felt her love for us as sisters on the journey with her toward the cross. She was beautiful, wise, and wonderful—she was our Qené!

I also found that love poured from her in the form of her writings. She seemed to write the very wisdom of God, born from years of ministry, and a life lived well for the Lord. Anyone reading her writings and following through with practicing the advice and wisdom found within them will be forever changed. I know, because her friendship has changed me.

Qené, I still pray the phonebook. I am still inspired by the encouragement and hope found in your stories. I am still, after these many years, encouraged and moved by your wisdom and grace. You are a treasure, a very special friend with a very special name and purpose. And you help and encourage me to trust God and love others no matter what.

I'm sure that as you read these pages she will do this for you also. Be blessed and encouraged, brothers and sisters, as you journey through this book and toward the author and finisher of our faith, with our lovely and gifted sister Qené!

—Donna Akuchie, pastor's wife and sister in Christ

With so many books on the market that have been written on encouragement, what makes this book different from any other book? I believe the difference is standing at death's door over a period of several weeks. It is the doctor explaining to the family that there was one last procedure to try because all the others had failed to render results.

The doctor came into Qené's hospital room and told the family if this last procedure didn't bring results, there was nothing left to try. The situation was so severe that the doctors were considering bringing her son home from Afghanistan to be with the family during her final hours.

During those several weeks of being at death's door, Jesus was present. Qené experienced a level of intimacy and encouragement that has altered her theology about encouragement. The experience so impacted her that while she was coming out of the medically induced coma, she never ceased from praying and lifting the needs of others before the Lord. Jesus's presence at death's door with Qené introduced her to a level of encouragement that she had never known. Death wasn't a threat, and there was no fear. Death fell in the shadow of the light of His encouragement.

Isn't that what encouragement does? It enlightens the situation of a troubled heart, sheds the light of hope, and exposes the manipulation of the enemy's presence. Qené's experience has shown her ways to reach the human heart through her words and her experience of being encouraged, even at death's door.

That is what makes this book different!

—Malcolm Burleigh, personal friend and brother in Christ

Dedication

For my sweet Pat,
because I always choose you.
Thank you for believing in me.
Thank you for loving me back to life.

Even when we were young teenagers, we always said,
"God has something special for us."
And so He does.
Something special is every single day with you.

Something special is our Terrific Trio,
P. J., Woodi, and Jené,
and their spouses, Sadi, Michele, and Brandon.
Something special is our Tremendous Ten:
Courtney, Colin, Linsey, James, Allison, Justin,
Isaac, Hailey, Natalie, and Ben.

Something special is forty-five years of a marriage blessed by God.
Thank you, Pat! I love you dearly!

Foreword

I'll never forget my first introduction to Qené Jeffers's writing. Her words crossed my computer screen at a time of tremendous crisis in my life—a perfect storm, one could say. As I read a story about her daughter's wedding dress, I sobbed onto my keyboard—pouring out all my fears and hurts to the Lord. I had found a safe harbor.

It was October 2006. My husband and I were on the cusp of marking our second anniversary serving on the home mission field of prison and prison aftercare ministry in New England. We loved the work and especially enjoyed getting to establish a new ministry, New Brothers Fellowship. NBF was unlike any other ministry in the region, so we had been working hard to spread the word, develop partnerships with local churches, raise volunteers, and establish our missionary support. Then, just as we were beginning to the feel the momentum rising in the spring of that year, my husband became gravely ill. Within a week, he was bedridden. Most ministry commitments had to be canceled. Plans to grow the work had to be abandoned. Anyone who saw him knew he was very sick, but we worked hard to keep up appearances. We were very afraid people would lose confidence in us if they thought Doug was too sick to continue. The skies were growing very dark.

Then the waves began to crash. New Brothers, not understanding how seriously ill Doug was, began to feel disappointed with him. Rumors began to swirl, and men started calling my husband and saying terrible, hurtful things. He had no response. One man came to our apartment, demanding to speak to him. There was no way Doug could come to the door, so I stood before this man and listened as he diminished my husband's character and ministry.

The life of a missionary is demanding enough on a good day, but with my husband's illness I found myself in an entirely different struggle, more intense than anything I had ever experienced. I had to be both mother and father to our daughter, both homemaker and man of the house. Add to that the fact that I was trying desperately, in my own strength, to sustain the ministry at such a critical time in its development, and you have the makings of a nervous breakdown. I was in a place of such deep, spiritual need, but there was no one at all to turn to for counsel or encouragement. No one was ministering to me.

This is when I encountered Q.'s Queue.

It was just a simple, green page—nothing fancy to it at all. No backgrounds or headers or graphics. I scanned through her posts until my eyes landed on the only photo, a picture of a young bride putting on her earrings. I started to read.

Eleven years ago, I thought it was just happenstance that led me this blog page that sleepless night. I had no idea who Q. was or all that she had experienced in life. I did not know the depth of her personal relationship with God or her vast knowledge of God's Word. I wasn't looking for an anointed writer, just a moderately talented one. It was the middle of the night. I wanted something good to read— entertaining writing with decent punctuation. That was the extent of my expectations.

As I began reading that first post, I was very engaged. *Ah, this is great,* I thought. *She actually knows how to write really well.* I couldn't stop reading. It was such a charming tale of a pastor's daughter. It was a sentimental story, I thought, but as I began relating to this young bride,

I stopped thinking and started feeling. I stopped analyzing and began experiencing.

Then as the anointing of God fell upon me penetrating my weary spirit, I read these words:

> "Oh, Daddy, Daddy. I'm so sorry. I did everything I knew to do, but my dress is dirty and stained, and it can't be cleaned."

I still weep when I read this. She had not even begun to explain the spiritual lesson, but the Holy Spirit was already at work! My spirit was crying out to my heavenly Father, "Daddy, Daddy! I'm doing everything I can, but I just can't fix this." That is not talented writing but anointed writing. A sweet story alone will not change a life forever. When you read Qené's writing, you will discover as I did that she is writing parables, not just telling stories.

You see, Qené uses her words to minister life and truth. Using stories about her real life in the real world, she wraps hard truths in so much godly compassion for her readers that we can accept her wisdom with open arms—even when it confronts our sin and unbelief. The Lord has gifted Qené as a writer, but she has given that gift to Him to use for His purposes. The result is a ministry that truly is life changing. It certainly has changed mine.

I have to confess. When I heard how sick Qené was last year, my first thought was for only me. "God, you can't take Q. away from me. What will I do?" While this may reflect my selfish nature, I hope it also proves the life-changing impact Q. has had on my life. Eleven years ago I prayed for a woman of God I could learn from, a woman who was living her life for Christ in such a way that I could follow her example. After reading that first post, I read through every old post and then waited eagerly each day for any new post she might share. Her words were a source of life and instruction. Now that they are in a book, I look forward to sharing them with every woman I know. Her ministry of words is a precious gift to the whole body of Christ.

My husband recovered from his illness, and the Lord sustained New Brothers Fellowship. We continue to serve as missionaries, and I continue to look for Q.'s posts on Facebook. I continue to be challenged by her testimony and encouraged by her ministry. It is a distinct privilege to play a small part in sharing her book with others. I am not the woman I was eleven years ago, and I am not the woman of God I desire to be, but who I am today is in large part the fruit of Qené Jeffers's ministry of words.

In Him Alone,

Caroline Gregan
Assistant Director
New Brother's Fellowship

Preface

The stories and prayers of *A Peace Unfettered* are a randomly written anthology of my faith and family. While they are in no particular arrangement, I've tried to order them by season, if not chronologically.

Scattered about you will find short prayers that may speak to your need, or perhaps I have spoken the words that are floundering within you. You are welcome to join your prayers with mine and to make them your own. It is a great pleasure to imagine that at the end of the day, you would bow your head with mine, all tucked in with Christ, and declare "Amen" as you close the book cover and turn off the lights.

This anthology begins and ends with a testimony. My understanding of religion and relationship with God are very unique to me, just as yours is to you. We each have our stories—our experiences of how and when we met and became friends with God. If you are not there yet and find yourself in a struggle between religion and relationship, I pray my story will help you see that a relationship with Jesus, our Savior, is a personal choice that each one of us must make. While it may seem unnecessary to you, if you claim the faith of your family or church, you must know that the choice to receive Christ remains a personal one. At some point that decision is yours. It is my deepest desire and prayer that as you turn the pages of *A Peace Unfettered*, you will hear God calling you to draw close. I am praying that as He draws near to you, the sound of His voice calling you to salvation will be loud and clear, and that your heart will gladly repent and receive Him.

We are not guaranteed even one more breath, which is something I recently learned in a near-death experience. The stories that came out of that experience are at the end of this book. As you read the testimony of what happened to me, please remember this one thing I know to be true: if you do not know Him now—you will not live with Him then.

Early on after my recovery, I determined that I would not waste my suffering—I vowed to share it with as many people as possible. My life is a miracle. And from beginning to end, I must tell you what Jesus did for me. In the mix of my family and faith, there's always a little fun. I hope you enjoy those stories too—I've put just a few of them in here for you.

The story has begun … won't you join me? You read. I'll pray and count it all joy that you are taking this journey with me.

Qené Jeffers
June 14, 2017

Acknowledgments

Taught at an early age by a diligent mother to say "Please" and "Thank you," those words roll easily out of my heart and mouth. They are often accompanied with a sincere smile, an engaging embrace, or a hearty handshake. However, putting pen to paper, I am struggling to find the words that will adequately express the deep gratitude I feel for the people who contributed in some way to this anthology, both the big and small of it.

To my numerous friends who read my bedtime stories on social media, thank you for your daily encouragement to put my ponderings and prose in a book. From the first day I spilled my heart onto the page and called it a post, you've assured me that I am giving voice to those very things you struggle with daily. Thank you for sharing your lives with me, and thank you for speaking into mine. You are each loved with an everlasting love.

To Sandy Fox for swooping in at the last minute and saving my day by sharing your expertise on a well-placed comma. I'm so grateful to you for your review of my manuscript. Thank you.

To our Terrific Trio, P. J. and Sadi, Woodi and Michele, and Jené and Brandon; and to our Tremendous Ten, Courtney, Colin, Linsey, James, Allison, Justin, Isaac, Hailey, Natalie, and Ben—you are my heart. You are the story of my life. With dozens of stories still in my hopper, some of our funnier moments may never find their way to print, but they are forever written in my heart and engraved in the laughter lines around my mouth. You are precious to me. Thank you for letting me tell our stories.

To my Pat—thank you for believing in me. Those three leather-bound notebooks finally spilled over into a book! Your encouragement and love have given me a beautiful, happy life, and now they have given me the dream of my heart—my very own book. Thank you, sweet Pat!

And to Phil Yeager, Reggie Adams, the editors and design team of WestBow Press, thank you for giving an old grandma like me the opportunity to tell the world a bedtime story. What a gift!

Introduction

"Is Momma's little girl not a fraidy-cat anymore?"

I know this might seem a silly thing for an eighty-year-old mother to say to her near sixty-year-old daughter, but my mother knew me. She knew that fear and fretting plagued me for most of my life, and she was certain the circumstance at hand would cause me much angst and worry.

The day she said this to me was a most unusual day in itself. Mom had just begun a journey with cancer that was nearing a swift end. The decision had been made to dismiss her from the hospital so that she could spend her last week of life at home. My usefulness in this traumatic situation was hindered in part because I don't drive. So, in an attempt to do something, anything, to help, I volunteered to spend the night at the lake house and prepare it for my mother's homecoming.

Bending over my mom's hospital bed to plant a kiss on her forehead, I said, "It is okay, Momma. I really want to do this for you."

Not wishing to cause her any undue concern, I didn't tell her that I already asked my husband to spend the night with me, suggesting he could rise early the next morning to make the long trip to his place of work. He too understood what a really big deal this was for me, and always being ready to relieve my anxiety and fears, he quickly agreed.

How about you, friend? Are you like me, fearful and fretful? Does anxiety have a death grip on your heart?

As you turn the pages of *A Peace Unfettered*, you will discover a lifelong search for a peace that passes all understanding. For some thirty-seven years, I have been writing the stories of my life—simple stories that God has used to grow my faith in Him. He has helped me apply the truth of His Word to my fret-filled days. From the beginning pages of the testimony of my salvation all the way through to the testimony of my miraculous healing from a near-death experience, God has been my faithful friend, my hiding place, and my sanctuary. He alone is the answer to all fearful thoughts. "For God hath not given us the spirit of fear, but of power, and of love, and of a sound mind" (2 Timothy 1:7).

I would be lying if I told you that I have this all figured out. Oh, yes! I do have my weak moments, even to this day! It takes determination, perseverance, and intentional action on my part to escape the dreadful clutch of the spirit of fear. It takes tucking into Christ, my Prince of Peace.

There is an old hymn written way back in the 1700s that I dearly love. In part, it holds the secret to a life free from the bondage of fear. The verse is from "Come Thou Fount of Every Blessing," and it always causes a tear or two to puddle in the corners of my eyes and slide down my cheeks …

Come Thou Fount of Every Blessing[1]
O to grace how great a debtor
Daily I'm constrained to be!
Let Thy goodness, like a fetter
Bind my wandering heart to Thee.
Prone to wander, Lord, I feel it,
Prone to leave the God I love;
Here's my heart, O take and seal it,
Seal it for Thy courts above.

There are so many things to be fearful of in our world today. Trouble is on every corner. Fear is rampant at every turn. Even God's Word tells us that in the last days people's hearts will fail them for fear. Men, women, and children have sought peace in all the wrong places— many placing their very lives in bondage to drugs, alcohol, and vices of every kind in their frantic search for seemingly elusive peace.

Oh, friend! If we are to be bound to anything, let our wandering hearts be bound to Christ! That fetter is a holy fetter for out of it flows a freedom and a peace unfettered by worry, fear, or the worst circumstance.

A peace unfettered. You know that's what you are looking for. I pray you find it in my stories about faith and family.

There is an old saying that peace is joy resting, and joy is peace dancing. I pray that every time you open the cover and turn these pages, you'll find yourself resting and dancing along with me.

Tell Them the Story of Jesus

My husband often says that the best way to tell others about salvation through Christ is to tell them the story of Jesus and what He has done in your life. I want to share that with you. It's my testimony.

My testimony actually begins long before I was born. As with many of you, family heritage and choices made by parents played a big part in who I am and how I would know God and worship Him.

My father's family is German and Catholic. They have a strong heritage in the Catholic Church, being very devout followers of the faith. My mother's family occasionally attended one of the local churches—Methodist, I think. However, when my mother married my father, she became a Catholic by taking instruction and baptism into the Catholic faith. She was very devout and perhaps stronger in her Catholic faith than my father, who spent his high school years in a Catholic boarding school in Kansas.

Because of my father's heritage in the Catholic Church and my mother's choice to join the faithful and practice Catholicism, I was born Catholic. I'm what is known as a cradle Catholic.

I was due to be born on August 15, 1954. August 15 just happens to be a holy day of obligation for Catholics. That's a day when all Catholics are obligated to attend Mass. The Assumption of the Blessed Virgin

Mary takes place on August 15, and Catholics believe that Mary, at the end of her earthly life, was taken into heaven, body and soul. This day of obligation was dogmatically defined (an infallible statement issued by a pope) by Pope Pius XII on November 1, 1950.

There are many Catholics who believe that Mary did not die but was taken to heaven, as were Enoch and Elijah. However, her death has not been dogmatically defined, so it is not an error to believe that she was taken to heaven while her earthly body was still alive. For Catholics, this date is known as her heavenly birthday.[2]

As it was a new teaching of the church, my parents had decided to name me Assumpta Qené if I was born on this feast day. I can only thank God all these years later for His divine intervention. He had all my days numbered even from the beginning of time, and my life was not to begin until August 18, three days later. I have always been very happy to be named Qené Manon Teresa Konen.

I was baptized in the Catholic Church when I was two weeks old and spent my growing-up years attending Mass every Sunday and catechism classes every Wednesday. They say that if a child is raised in the church until age seven, they will always be faithful and never leave their Catholic faith. All those years ago, that certainly was said of me.

I loved the Catholic Church. I loved the ritual, the Mass, the celebration of the Eucharist, the rosary, the stations of the cross, the incense, the holy water, and meatless Fridays. I loved speaking Latin during the Mass, and although I didn't know what it meant, I could speak the Mass in Latin by heart. I especially loved the nuns.

I was a very religious person. As a young girl, I wanted to be a nun, and I spent many hours making my habit by wrapping myself in long, flowing curtains to become the bride of God, pressing out little rounds of bread with pill bottles to make communion wafers, and carrying an empty toilet paper roll pretending it was a candle.

I was a terribly shy and backward child, so backward that my kindergarten teacher told my mother not to expect much out of me because she believed that I was retarded. I was so shy that I thought I would never be married, and I wanted to spend my life as a nun, preferably as a cloistered nun who was shut away with prayers and penance.

Back in the 1950s, things were done in the old way. Mass was said in Latin, and women and girls were expected to have their heads covered when entering the church. We had a closet in our home located in the little bathroom. The closet was beside the toilet, and it is where we kept our church hats. We loved that little closet!

When it was time to go to Mass, my sisters and I would race to the bathroom to see who could be the first to find the special hat, the favorite hat, the one with a long pheasant feather attached to it. The winner would proudly sport it on her head, making sure that in the car and the pew she would turn her head just so and brush the feather against the face of a sister, perhaps even giving her a poke in the eye with the beloved long feather.

There was always a sister that refused to wear a hat if she couldn't have the beloved beige tam with the feather. And there was always a sister that would lose her hat to the open toilet while trying to wrestle and grab for the eye-poking feather.

We would often arrive at the church only to discover that someone had left their hat at home due to hurt feelings or a hat swimming in the toilet. So, making a mad dash to the bathroom in the basement of the church, my mother would bobby-pin a square of toilet paper firmly and painfully into the erring sister's hair, making a hat of sorts that would satisfy our obligation.

In the 1960s, after Vatican II when a lot of changes were made in the Catholic Church, we were no longer required to wear a hat in church.

Our priest at the time, who was a very dear family friend, said that the pope had taken pity on the poor little Konen girls and made the new ruling so we wouldn't have to wear toilet paper on our heads to Mass. We were relieved, but we were also sad, as that meant we no longer had a hat closet or a beige-colored tam with a long pheasant feather to fight over.

When I was a sixth grader, I fell in love with a boy named Pat. The minute I saw him, I knew that he would be an important person in my life. But I was just too shy to meet boys and have a boyfriend; it was easier to hide behind a nun's habit.

I still remember our first meeting all those years ago at the corner of McCord and Valley Streets riding our bikes with our friends. I still remember it because even at the young age of twelve, I knew that this person, this Pat, was going to be someone special in my life. That brief moment at the corner of McCord and Valley was the beginning of a beautiful life for me.

Pat moved away from Neosho but returned a couple of years later. We met again when I was a freshman in high school at age fourteen. We were both enrolled in drama class, and once I overcame my shyness, in our high school years together, we were inseparable!

A few weeks after our first date, while Pat was walking me home from school, he began telling me about his dreams for the future. That very week, he had made plans to enlist in the Navy following graduation. It was the dream of his heart and the tradition of his family. It's the way it would be.

"If we still know each other when I get back from boot camp, I will stop by to show you my uniform," he said.

What? Are you crazy? I thought. *I will always know you.* He was the dream of my heart, and I knew that's the way it would be. Isn't it funny how a freeze-frame moment in time can change your life in such a dramatic way?

Pat was not Catholic. At that time, he was not anything, although he had been saved and baptized in the Baptist Church. He didn't attend church or even talk much about his faith. In fact, he was running from a special call on his life, and I wouldn't even know about that until many years later after we were married and had three children.

I had two strikes against me, coming from a Catholic home and coming from a broken home. Neither was popular in that day. My parents divorced when I was a freshman in high school, about the same time I began dating Pat. His family was concerned about both of those issues, but we were in love and determined that nothing could separate us. I did tell him, though, not to ask me to leave the Catholic Church, as I would have to choose it over him.

We were married in St. Agnes Catholic Church in Springfield, Missouri, on August 26, 1972. Pat's family wasn't eager to attend the wedding Mass, and in fact, there were very few members of his family there. But I determined that our ceremony would be during the celebration of the Mass. I was sure none of his family had ever attended, and I thought it would be good for them to see why my Catholic faith was so important to me. Pat's brothers were in our wedding, and they had fun shocking the priest by drinking the holy water and ducking the drops of water during the blessing when the priest sprinkled us with holy water. They clearly didn't understand anything about the Catholic Church—the holiness of the ritual nor the importance of the sacrament.

It was a fun, beautiful day, though very hot. The brothers managed to find an old wheelbarrow, and our priest provided one of his vestments to put in the bottom of it so my dress wouldn't get dirty when the chivalry took place. On that hot day, with my groom in dress blues, Pat pushed me down Jefferson Street in that wheelbarrow. It is one of my favorite wedding memories.

When Pat and I married, he was in the United States Navy. He had just completed a nine-month West-Pac cruise and came home the week before our wedding. In the Catholic Church at that time, it was a requirement that the wedding take place in a Catholic church and the banns of marriage announced at least three Sundays before the wedding. The banns of marriage are simply an announcement that a wedding will take place for a man and woman on a certain date. It allows everyone the opportunity to attend the wedding so if anyone knows of any legal objections, the marriage will be stopped.[3]

Before the marriage takes place, the Catholic party must also attest to his or her intention of not leaving the Catholic Church and promise to baptize and raise the children in the Catholic faith. The non-Catholic party is informed of these promises, attests to understanding these promises, and in turn promises not to interfere in their fulfillment. Proper preparation must be made when a person marries a non-Catholic, so a time of instruction for the couple is required before the ceremony.[4] Due to Pat coming home only the week before our wedding, the priest had one day for our instruction. He showed us a film about marriage in the Catholic Church, asked if we had any questions, and helped us plan the service regarding scriptures, the vows, and music. That was it. Pat felt very, very lucky. He had dodged the bullet of Catholic instruction.

Following the wedding, we moved to San Diego where his ship was based. Unfortunately, within weeks of our moving to San Diego, Pat was sent to Vietnam. He had time to bring me home over a weekend before the ship pulled out of port. After he left, I discovered I was expecting a baby, and he got to hear the good news over the telephone. We were both very excited, thinking that the baby would arrive about the same time that he would arrive in home port. But early December I lost our baby through miscarriage. It was a devastating loss, one that I still feel to this day.

The Red Cross contacted Pat's ship and requested, by order of my doctor, that Pat be allowed to come home on emergency leave for a month. I was very nervous about Pat traveling. It seemed that staying at work on his ship was much safer than traveling through Da Nang and Saigon by air flight. God's hand was surely on our lives during that two-week trip home. The generosity of a helicopter pilot to transport Pat instead of the scheduled flight on a mail plane very likely saved his life. The mail plane was shot down, and the entire crew went missing. But Pat made it home safe and sound, and we got to spend our first Christmas together.

Pat returned to Vietnam after the holidays and spent many months sweeping the Vietnam harbor for mines. Three different times, his return to the States was delayed. I tried not to worry, and I was relieved and thankful when he returned safely home the week of our first wedding anniversary. It was a long and painful first year!

While Pat was gone, I lived with several different family members. I stayed with my aunt in Kansas City for several months, helping her care for a four-year-old and a new baby; I stayed a few weeks with my mother and siblings at their home in Springfield, but it was very hard going back to the family routine with them now that I was married. I also spent several months with my in-laws. Out of respect for them, I would go to Mass on Saturday evenings or very early Sunday mornings, and I would then attend church services with them at a local Baptist church.

We were brought up to believe it was sin for us to actively participate in any other religious activity or service outside the Catholic Church.[5] So, I didn't sing the hymns, and I didn't listen to the sermon. All I did was attend the service, and I enjoyed many of the people I met there, but I was very careful not to take part in their worship. All these years later I know they meant well, but at the time I was very put off by the looks they shared when I entered the church building. The pointing and staring and the silently mouthed words, "Pray for her. She's Catholic, you know." It hardened my heart to know they were so critical of my Catholic faith. And as I look back, I wonder—why didn't they "follow the way of love?" (1 Corinthians 14:1 NIV)

After Pat's discharge from the Navy, we moved back home to Neosho. Between June 1975 and October 1978, I had three babies! Each one was baptized in the Catholic Church just as I promised.

Those were very poor years for us with many job changes and low pay with no health insurance. Two of my babies were delivered by C-section, and my recovery time was slow due to having the babies so close together. When the youngest baby was one year old, I contracted a staph infection in my eyes. Overnight I became very ill, and unbeknownst to me, that was the beginning of my journey to a personal relationship with Christ.

I woke up late that morning. It was past time to get my oldest son up and dressed for preschool. In fact, he had already missed the school bus. I threw on some clothes, dressed the kids, poured cereal to eat in the car, and we headed out the door and on our way. I didn't feel well. I had a headache and felt feverish. When we reached the school, I got all the kids out of the car, which seemed to take more energy than I had that day, and we proceeded down the hall to P. J.'s classroom. On the way, a few people greeted me with concerned looks on their faces. Everyone asked me if I was feeling okay. I thought that was odd, since you generally can't tell by looking that someone has a headache, but I smiled and said I was fine and delivered my boy safely into the hands of the preschool teacher. Upon arriving home, I went in the bathroom to comb my hair and properly dress for the day. When I looked in the mirror, I was utterly shocked! My forehead and eyes were very swollen and turned black! No one had said anything other than "Are you feeling okay?" I couldn't believe how bad I looked! I began to cry.

It was obvious that I needed to see the doctor, but I had no money, no insurance, and no one to care for my children. By this time I was feeling sick, and I didn't think I could take them with me, even if I found the money to go. I called a friend from high school who happened to live in our town. She and I often watched each other's children, so I was hoping she could help me. Her husband is a doctor and unexpectedly he was home! I told him my symptoms over the phone and asked if there was some medicine I could take over-the-counter. I didn't have money to go to the clinic. He told me in no uncertain terms that I was to go to the doctor's office immediately. He said to tell the receptionist that he had insisted I come.

My friend was out for the day, and she was unable to watch my children while I went to my appointment. I called Pat's mom, and she was unable to help me. My mother lived in Arizona, and I had no other family available. I tried calling every friend I had, and no one could help that day. I was beside myself with what to do!

I decided to take a bath and see if that would help me feel better. While I was in the tub, I was sobbing and begging God to send me help. I didn't know what to do! No sooner had that prayer escaped my lips than Pat was standing there in the doorway! Someone had called a bomb threat into the factory where he worked, and they had sent everyone home! I was so glad to see him. He helped me with the children and took me to the doctor. I was sent home with medicine and told to go to the ER if my symptoms worsened. Hours later I could feel the swelling spread across my face, and my fever spiked to 105 degrees. I was very, very sick. A friend in our neighborhood was having a dinner party, but she generously offered to keep our children so that my worried Pat could take me to the hospital. I was there for a week running a high fever, and my eyes and forehead were swollen and black. It was a very dangerous infection, and it was only by God's hand that I didn't die or at the very least lose my eyesight. I did lose all my eyelashes, and even forty years later I am reminded of that by the sparse lashes that frame my eyes.

Shortly after that illness, I went into a major clinical depression. My poor health, hectic lifestyle with three young children, and very often never enough money for groceries caused me a great deal of stress and anxiety. I was very self-sufficient and overwhelmed with all I had to do to take care of my children and home. I often overextended myself by helping others with various needs. In fact, a newspaper article was written about my volunteer work, which stated that I was known as the woman who never said no.

Back then we often talked about baby blues following the births of our children. At the very least, I thought that's what was wrong with me. Today, I'm confident I would have been diagnosed with full-blown postpartum depression. A friend referred me to a therapist, assuring me that he would help me even without insurance. It was hard for me to make that appointment. I never admitted how severe my depression was to my Pat, and now he was sure to find out.

My depression was severe, and the therapist thought it was necessary for me to be hospitalized, but again we had no money, no insurance, and three babies ages one to four years old without anyone to care for them. I was able to convince the doctor that the stress of going to the hospital would be too much to bear and only add to my burden and depression. I didn't want to leave my children and Pat. So, it was decided that I could be treated with medication and frequent counseling. After several months of both, I began to feel better and was able to cope with my life. I slowly learned to stay within my limits of what I was able to do. I learned to say no.

Pat seemed content to go to Mass with me in the early years of our marriage. We were youth leaders at our local parish, and interestingly enough, the priest who officiated our marriage was now assigned to this parish. I also taught the third and fourth grade catechism class on Sunday mornings.

During the severest weeks of my depression, I began seeking a deeper relationship with God. I knew that my life was too much for me to handle on my own, though for several years I had tried to do just that. I knew God was the answer to all of my problems and that I would only be able to find peace in my religion. I began going to Mass every day with all of my children in tow, much to the dismay of the elderly congregants. We sat in front so that they wouldn't have to turn around to see what my children were doing.

One day while looking through some family pictures and mementos, I came across a prayer card to the Virgin Mary. It told the many ways Mary would intercede and bless if a particular written prayer was prayed every day. I was very excited about it, and I believed it to be true. It's what I'd been taught all my life. A friend named Zee stopped by to see me that day, and I very excitedly showed her the card. She said, "Qené, that sounds very nice, and it would be wonderful if those good things could happen in your life, but they are not going to happen from you praying this prayer. Do you believe the Bible is God's Word?" I said yes. She said, "Nowhere in the Bible does it tell us to pray to Mary. Nowhere does it say that she can intercede for us. The Word is very clear. Jesus is the only mediator we have. He is the only one who can intercede for us."

Zee wrote some scriptures out for me to read. After she had left my house that day, I was very disappointed and confused. I had never read the Bible, but I certainly believed that everything I was taught was in the Word. Only the priest read the scriptures. I had no idea how to look up anything in the Bible. I did a little research and found out that this belief in prayers to Mary and her authority to intercede for us is based on a tradition of the church. In fact, I learned many of the doctrines in the Catholic Church are based on traditions and are not scripturally founded. I soon discovered that the traditions of the faith are considered to be as authoritative as the scriptures. But, how could that be—especially when the traditions of the church aren't confirmed in the Word of God?

As I began drawing closer to God, I started checking books out of the library about faith in God. One of the books I read was a daily devotion book by Norman Vincent Peale. It was very helpful to me and often talked about reading the Bible. Once or twice I tried to read our family Catholic Bible, but I thought it was like a regular book and that you had to start at the beginning. I never made it much past the first two or three chapters in Genesis.

Since we were taught that only the priest could interpret the scriptures, we were not encouraged to read the Bible on our own. Of course, the scriptures were read in Mass, but early on that was in Latin. We did have a family Bible, but it was not one that was ever read. It was put away for safekeeping. I had absolutely no knowledge of the scriptures. One day while Pat and I took a vacation day and attended Mass at a church in Eureka Springs, I saw a beautiful banner hanging in the church that said, "Come unto me all you who labor and are heavy-hearted, and I will give you rest." It was so beautiful and spoke so clearly to my need that I started crying. I had never heard that saying before, but I knew this was the rest that I needed and wanted. This is what I was looking for! I read it over and over again during the service—I had to memorize it so that I could find out if these words were in the Bible.

When we arrived home, I called Pat's mom and asked about it. She told me that those words are in the Bible. These are words spoken by Jesus. Maxine also told me how to find it in the Bible. I printed it out by hand and put it on my refrigerator door because I wanted to read it often. Those words were like a soothing ointment to my broken spirit and my tired body.

Because Norman Vincent Peale talked so much about the scriptures in this book I was reading, I decided to start reading the Bible for myself. Pat's parents had bought us The Living Bible (a paraphrase) for Christmas, and I found it easier to read than my Catholic Bible. I don't know why, other than God's guidance, but I started reading the book of Romans. I read all of it. I didn't understand all of it, but I read enough to be shocked at what it said about salvation. A person must believe in his or her heart and confess with his or her mouth, and all who call on the name of the Lord Jesus will be saved from eternal punishment for their sin—from hell.

"Yes, all have sinned; all fall short of God's glorious ideal" (Romans 3:23 TLB).

"For the wages of sin is death, but the free gift of God is eternal life through Jesus Christ our Lord" (Romans 6:23 TLB).

"For Moses wrote that if a person could be perfectly good and hold out against temptation all his life and never sin once, only then could he be pardoned and saved. But the salvation that comes through faith says, "You don't need to search the heavens to find Christ and bring him down to help you," and "You don't need to go among the dead to bring Christ back to life again."

For salvation that comes from trusting Christ—which is what we preach—is already within easy reach of each of us; in fact, it is as near as our own hearts and mouths. For if you tell others with your own mouth that Jesus Christ is your Lord and believe in your own heart that God has raised Him from the dead, you will be saved. For it is by believing in his or her heart that a person becomes right with God; and with his or her mouth he or she tells others of his or her faith, confirming his or her salvation.

For the scriptures tell us that no one who believes in Christ will ever be disappointed. Jew and Gentile are the same in this respect: they all have the same Lord who generously gives His riches to all those who ask Him for them. Anyone who calls upon the name of the Lord will be saved" (Romans 10:5–13 TLB).

I had never heard anything like that before! I thought I was a Christian because I was Catholic. I didn't know that the Bible stated it was a personal choice that I had to make. I thought the church claimed my salvation for me because I was a member, baptized when I was two weeks old. My parents had decided that for me, and their faith was my faith. What an eye-opener to discover that I am personally accountable to God!

That day, in my home, with my babies asleep for their naps, my heart was changed when I asked Jesus to be my Savior and to help me live my life. Other than my sobs for God to help me the day I was so sick, I had never prayed a prayer that wasn't written or memorized. But that day I told Him how miserable and confused and tormented I was about my life, and I needed His help and strength to live my life and raise my children. I wanted to be a good wife and mother. I wanted a peaceful heart. I was beginning to understand that I needed and wanted His free gift of salvation, which was made possible by Jesus's death on the cross and His resurrection three days later.

I didn't realize the implication of all I had done. I just knew that instantly I felt like a new person, with a new life, but I didn't know I was supposed to tell anyone or even how to do that. I didn't understand that what happened to me was called getting saved. I just knew that I had made an about face—instead of pursuing the things of God with a religious heart, I was now pursuing Him through a personal relationship. I wanted to know Him.

In the Catholic Church, there is no opportunity to tell people about an experience like that. And my friends at the church wouldn't have understood the getting saved thing either. We thought we were Christians because we were Catholic. But now, suddenly I knew I was different inside, and I could feel God's presence in my life in a way that I never had before. So as God began to draw me closer to Him, I began seeking Him in the Mass every day. That was all I knew to do!

I found out about a marriage encounter weekend through my priest. I was very eager to go. It was a weekend designed to improve communication in your marriage, and there was so much that Pat and I needed to talk about! Even though we had a wonderful, loving relationship, we sometimes struggled with communication. I managed to talk my husband into going to the encounter weekend, and my friend from high school agreed to watch our three children.

While I was there at the encounter, I was given a chance to go to confession. During my confession, I shared with the priest that I had sinned when my last child was born. The doctor said it was dangerous for me to have another baby, and I decided to allow him to do the necessary surgery while they were doing the C-section so that I could no longer have babies. I talked about that at some length with the priest, and he did help me let go of my guilt for having done that.

I also told him that I had started going to a local Baptist church on Sunday nights, and there was a Bible study on the book of Romans that I wanted to attend during the day. I really wanted to go to a Bible study on Psalms that was being held at the Catholic church, but they didn't provide babysitting, and the Baptist church did. I asked permission to attend the study at the Baptist church. The priest said this to me, "I think it would be fine for you to go. However, just be careful that you don't lose your Catholic faith." Later I thought to myself, *That is so odd! I never would have thought it was possible to lose my Catholic faith while studying the Bible, God's Word!*

I began attending the Bible study on Tuesday mornings and would occasionally go to Sunday evening worship with my mother-in-law. Pat wouldn't attend the worship service with me—he stayed home, took care of the kids, and watched reruns of the Robert Schuller at the Crystal Cathedral worship service on television.

I didn't know it, but God was working in Pat's life too. Within a few short weeks, God would take my husband and my family through a very alarming accident. It shook him to the core. It shook us all—I still get chills when I think about it.

It was a cold, rainy night, and Pat was working late. He was a driver for a local bread company in Joplin, Missouri. The day had started out as a beautiful day, so he rode his motorcycle to work. Later in the day, the weather changed to a cold rain. Coming home late on that cold, rainy night was very poor judgment, but he didn't want me to get the kids out so late to pick him up in the car. So, he started the twenty-mile trip home on his motorcycle.

It was about 8:30 p.m., and I was home getting the children ready for bed. We were getting a late start because we had been waiting for Pat to come home for dinner. I finally decided to put the children in the bathtub all together to make it quick work. After they had been in for several minutes, my oldest son P. J. came running into the living room naked and wet. "Momma," he said, "Daddy fell off his motorcycle, and he's all wet." I smacked his little bottom and sent him back to the tub, telling him that his dad was okay and would be home soon expecting him to be bathed and in bed. The truth is that my young son had a premonition about what was happening to his daddy …

Several minutes later I heard a car in the driveway. I looked out the window and saw Pat and his boss getting out of a car. At first, I was irritated at Pat for bringing his boss to the house so late! My house was a mess, my kids were in the bathtub, and he was late! But then I noticed that Pat was limping badly, and I ran to open the door. He was very shaken and told me that he'd been involved in a terrible accident several blocks from where he worked. A semitruck had passed him on the wet road, and the draft from the truck blew his windbreaker up over his head!

Unable to see, he lost control of his motorcycle, and the bike slid under the rear wheels of the semitruck with him still on it. The tires ran over the gas tank of his bike and then flipped him off and out from under the truck. Pat slid down the highway on his backside and then very suddenly found himself standing at the side of the road. Amazing—an absolutely amazing miracle. He didn't tell me this part until weeks later, but he took his helmet off and said, "God, I hear you!"

The man who was driving behind him had witnessed the whole thing. He thought Pat was surely dead and couldn't believe his eyes when the mist cleared and he saw Pat standing at the side of the road. It was, he said, a miracle! The next day a friend of ours who was a highway patrolman stopped by the house. He said, "Pat, there were two other accidents last night that happened just as your accident happened. We carried both of those boys away in body bags." We were both shaken to the core. A trip to the ER would reveal a broken tailbone and a few bruises but nothing more.

A few weeks later God spoke to me about something. It wasn't an audible voice, and yet I heard Him speaking very clearly in my thoughts and my heart.

Pat was looking into the opportunity to go to college using his GI money for education. It was a way for us to have some money for our family and for him to get an education and possibly a better job. He didn't know what he wanted to do or what he wanted to study. One evening while I was stirring spaghetti on the stove, God spoke in my heart and said, "Pat is supposed to be a preacher. He's supposed to study to be a preacher." How odd! How could this be? Yes, I was walking close to God and had that experience of asking Jesus to be my Savior, but I was still in the Catholic Church. I was still attending Mass every day. How could Pat be a preacher and help me with the youth in the Catholic church at the same time? How could he be a Baptist pastor with me still being Catholic?

When Pat got home from work that night, I said, "I think I know what you are supposed to go to school for. You are supposed to study to be a preacher." His eyes were big, his mouth was gaping, and he said, "You know, I've been thinking about that all day!"

Pat had never told me that when he was twelve-years-old, he felt God calling him to preach during a vacation Bible school. He had made a public profession of that during Bible school, but within a year or two completely ignored his calling and stopped going to church. To cinch the deal, he simply denied his calling by marrying a little Catholic girl who had said she would never leave the Catholic Church.

During the following weeks, I attended the Bible study on Romans taught by the pastor, Brother Tom Casady. Through the study and under the direction of a visiting evangelist during a revival service at the church, I finally understood what had happened in my heart! When Brother Tom said, "Missy, when are you going to be ready to make your decision for Christ?" I finally knew this was a place where I could make my personal profession of faith in Christ. I couldn't wait for the revival service that night so that I could go forward during the invitation and tell everyone what had happened to me! I wanted to be baptized—I understood that it would be a picture of what had taken place in my heart, and I couldn't wait to do that. It would be a picture of the death, burial, and resurrection of Jesus Christ. Brother Tom said that through my baptism, I would be preaching a sermon—giving a testimony of all that God had done and was doing in my life. It was so exciting, and I felt so good about my decision!

A week later when I was to be baptized, two very hard things happened to discourage me in my new life with Christ. The first was that I had to tell my priest what happened, and I needed to resign from my catechism class. My husband was going to be a pastor. My dream as a little girl of becoming a nun was now unfolding in a much different way than I ever expected. I was going to be a pastor's wife! I was confused about many things during that time. How could I go to church all my life and not understand that scripture says I need to make a personal decision to follow Christ? My parents chose to baptize me at two weeks old, but according to the Bible my heritage in the church didn't matter. It was a personal choice that I had to make, and somehow I missed making that connection! Then I realized I had been following the church, not Christ. I was a religious person and nothing more. Even when I was confirmed in the church at age eight, that was a decision by someone else. Everyone in our catechism class was confirmed at the same time—it wasn't a choice we personally made.

The second thing that happened to discourage me took place when I called my mother to invite her to my baptism. I was afraid to call her, but I knew I must. I told her that I had been saved, and I was going to be baptized in the Baptist Church. I really wanted her to come to my baptism. She said, "But Qené, why would you need to be baptized? You were baptized when you were two weeks old." I told her that this time I was being baptized because I chose to; before I was baptized because she and Daddy chose it for me. I was trying to be obedient to Christ, and I wanted to be baptized to show my new relationship with Him. She refused to come.

And I felt guilty. Guilty for turning my back on the church. Guilty for disrupting the local parish. Guilty for rebelling against my parents and their choice for me. Guilty for not teaching my third and fourth graders. How could such a happy time in my life be filled with so much guilt and pain?

It was very hard for me emotionally over the next few months. It took a few years before I let go of that guilt feeling. I knew what I had done was right. I knew that I had pleased God. But it was still hard. Being Catholic was as much a part of me as being a woman or being white. It was who I was; it was part of my identity. I had to go back to counseling for several months. I felt myself slipping back into that awful depression. The emotions of joy and excitement over my new life in Christ were conflicting with my feelings of betrayal and guilt over leaving the Catholic Church. I needed to resolve this so I could enjoy my new life in Christ and do what He had called me to do—serve in ministry alongside my husband.

My husband and I have now been serving in Baptist churches for the past thirty-seven years. I have come a long way in my walk with Christ. Every day I learn something new about Him. My goal for these past many years has simply been to be faithful, available, and teachable. My life verse has been the motto for my walk with Him:

> "[For my determined purpose is] that I may know Him [that I may progressively become more deeply and intimately acquainted with Him, perceiving and recognizing and understanding the wonders of His Person more strongly and more clearly] and that I may, in the same way, come to know the power outflowing from His resurrection [which it exerts over believers], and that I may so share His sufferings as to be continually transformed [in spirit into His likeness even] to His death, [in the hope]" (Philippians 3:10 AMPC).

It has been a wonderful, beautiful life with Him, and I look forward to all He will allow me to do and experience in the time to come. My testimony will never end because I have shared my faith in Christ with many friends and family, and they too have believed in Christ to save them from their sin.

My testimony gives proof to the statement that God is in the business of changing hearts—even a religious heart that follows hard after the traditions of men. We must remember that He is the one who does the work. Only the Holy Spirit could have brought me conviction and understanding that He wants to have a personal relationship with me. A religious heart cannot be won over with sharp criticism and condemnation. It is only through God's Word that we ever know Him because He is the Word. We must follow the way of love with truth.

My heritage as a cradle-Catholic gives me a different perspective on all things concerning the church. I do hold those memories dear. I do love Christ with all my heart. I do love being a pastor's wife. And I'm so grateful for the many opportunities He gives me each day to minister to people and share my faith.

After forty-five years of marriage, I am still very grateful to God for the one He chose to be my beloved husband. Even as young teenagers we knew that God had something special for our life together. And, indeed, He does!

"For I know the thoughts that I think toward you, saith the LORD, thoughts of peace, and not of evil, to give you an expected end" (Jeremiah 29:11).

I Once Was Blind

Many years ago, I was blind. I was living in a darkness that cannot be described. There was no light. No color. No beauty. There was nothing but darkness that enveloped the whole of my life. I was miserable and desperate. I was blind and condemned. I could not see any hope of ever escaping the pitch-black darkness.

Many people knew I was blind, but they refused to help me. They watched me struggle on a daily basis, minute by minute trying to make my way along in the darkness. They never offered a hand to guide me. They never offered love in compassion and understanding. Instead, they saw my blindness and chose to curse and ridicule me. They reproved and rebuked me again and again until my heart grew hard and cold against them. They used their religion as a club to beat me, pounding away at my flesh until I was weak and ashamed. I bore my shame as I bore their judgment. It weighed heavy on my shoulders as I struggled against its enormous weight.

Day after day, trudging through the darkness with what seemed to be the weight of the world on my back, I grew weak and weary. I longed for someone to rescue me from my darkness and shame, from the cruel judgment of my self-righteous tormentors. I needed someone to rescue me from myself. As each day passed and no help came, I grew bitter and lonely, even despairing of life itself.

But one day I was greeted by one who is light. He used a simple conversation with one of His daughters to open my eyes and show me the way. He led her to follow the way of love. She listened to my heart and heard my pitiful cries. She wiped tears from my eyes and washed my feet. She spoke truth into my life and hope into my heart.

Then the one who is light gave me "...beauty for ashes, the oil of joy for mourning, the garment of praise for the spirit of heaviness; that they might be called a tree of righteousness, the planting of Jehovah, that He might be glorified" (Isaiah 61:3).

I shall forever be grateful to Him, my Jesus.

And I shall forever be grateful to Zee for following the way of love.

"And now these three remain; faith, hope, and love. But the greatest of these is love. Follow the way of love ..." (1 Corinthians 13:13; Corinthians 14:1 NIV).

Words That Become Like Eagles

I just want to share a few words with you today that will speak to your heart in a special way. Words that will perhaps shock you by their straightforwardness and simplicity, or words that will at least awaken and alert you to consider yourself and the condition of your soul.

I just want to share a few words that will unite and blend to echo in your mind. A melody that will bounce against the walls of the world to bring a smile to young and old alike.

Words that become like eagles to mount up and fly like the wind within your soul, soaring upward and onward having no limits.

I just want to share a few words with you today that will break your heart. Words so gentle and sweet that no ear could turn away, that no heart could not be touched. I want tears to form in your eyes as these words pierce you, break you, heal you, and rebuild you.

I want to share a few words with you today that will make a difference in the rest of your life—if you will let them. Words that will give you comfort and strength. Powerful words that will save your soul. I just want to share with you words that are life.

"In the beginning was the Word and the Word was with God, and the Word was God" (John 1:1).

"And the Word was made flesh and dwelt among us, (and we beheld His glory, the glory of the only begotten of the Father), full of grace and truth" (John 1:14).

I just want to share with you today the Word who is "the same yesterday, and today and, forever"—Jesus Christ! (Hebrews 13:8)

Are You a Fraidy-Cat?

I have a tendency to be a fraidy-cat.

My earliest memory of being afraid was when I was three years old. I was being put to bed by my mother in my bright red bedroom, which was decorated with a cardboard circus train hanging on the wall. That particular night I cried hysterically because I was just sure that the lion caged on the train was going to escape and eat me up while the rest of the family slept soundly in their beds. I remember that my mother made many, many trips into the room that night trying to soothe me and comfort me, but finally she had all she could take, and her hysteria became greater than mine. Screaming like a crazy woman, she entered the red room and ripped the circus train off the wall, threatening me if I made one more sound. I didn't. I didn't dare. I'm not sure who I was more afraid of, the lion who was already halfway out of his cage when my mother ripped him off the wall, or her …

I have a tendency to be a fraidy-cat.

So, I *never* watch scary movies. I didn't allow my children to watch them either. Freddy Krueger never once set foot in my house; he never even made it onto the front porch. I've always believed that whatever you put into your heart and your mind is what you live with. If you don't put scary things in there, then you won't be scared! That makes perfect sense to me. And I don't like being scared ... so, I'm careful to guard my heart and mind from the likes of Freddy Krueger and all of his scary friends! No monsters, no mass murderers, no deranged freaks, and no little-girl-eating lions riding in a circus train will ever make their way into my heart!

I have a tendency to be a fraidy-cat.

All my friends know that I won't watch scary movies, so they just assumed when my husband traveled to Belarus on an eighteen-day mission trip that I would be too afraid to stay home alone. They were wrong. I wasn't afraid to be in my home alone. My home is a place love and joy, blessing and favor, peace unfettered that runs like a river, and rest. Nothing to be scared about here! And since I don't hide scary movies in my heart and mind, there is nothing to be afraid of. I don't live with fear.

But ... I have a tendency to be a fraidy-cat.

The fear that grips my heart is a little more ominous than Freddy Krueger. It sneaks into my heart by first sneaking into my mind. And before it fills my mind with fear, it fills my mind with doubt and questions—perhaps with the same doubts and questions that you have.

Will the Lord ever answer my prayer? Does He even hear my prayer? If He doesn't hear my prayer or answer my prayer, is He really there? Does He really care about the things that worry me and concern me? Does He care when money is tight or when there is none? Does He care that we struggle with physical pain and ailments and that our loved ones are dying? Does He care that people all around the world are unemployed and children are starving? Does He care that orphans and widows are lonely, with no one to care for them? Will the war ever be won? Will evil be destroyed, and will soldiers be returned safely home? Will our children be safe at school? Will they fit in, and have godly friends? What do we do when there's no health insurance and someone is sick? Does God care about gas prices? Does He see His children being persecuted and murdered? Will this world ever know peace?

These questions are what make us fraidy-cats. Satan, the great deceiver, has carefully planted each seed of doubt and worry in our minds. Before long it grows into a huge tree of fear with roots that reach deep into our hearts. But our Father knows that we are easily frightened by all these things and that we worry about tomorrow before its time has come. He gives us assurance with these words:

> "Let your character or moral disposition be free from love of money [including greed, avarice, lust, and craving for earthly possessions] and be satisfied with your present [circumstances and with what you have]; for He [God] Himself has said, I will not in any way fail you nor give you up nor leave you without support. [I will] not, [I will] not, [I will] not in any degree leave you helpless nor forsake nor let you down (relax My hold on you)! [Assuredly not!] So we take comfort and are encouraged and confidently and boldly say, The Lord is my Helper; I will not be seized with alarm [I will not fear or dread or be terrified]. What can man do to me?" (Hebrews 13:5–6 AMPC)

Isn't that just great? He will not, He will not, He will not in any way leave us helpless! He will not, He will not, He will not relax His hold on us! Don't you feel comforted, encouraged, confident, and bold because of His love for us?

Join me in declaring, "The Lord is my Helper; I will NOT be seized with alarm!"

When the day is spent, and all that's left is the strength for nighttime prayer, if your house is a home of peace and rest, there is no need to check under the bed for monsters or cardboard lions. I pray you will join me in resting well. I'm resting in Him!

Hidden with Christ in God

I've spent a lot of time in the past sixty-three years hiding. Growing up as the second child in a family of six, there was a lot to hide from. We played the typical outdoor hiding games of hide and seek and sardines, taking them indoors as needed due to rain, snow, and darkness. We added the likes of button, button when the younger children played.

We could play those games for hours! And we'd get so, so dirty doing it. No place was sacred when it came to hiding, and only one place was haunted, so we had dozens of great hiding places. Under brush, in the bushes, behind trees, in trees, up trees, the porch, the garage, the coal bin, the trellis—we could be anywhere or everywhere, often changing places when the seeker would get hot.

I remember playing a hiding game indoors on a rainy day with my sisters. I had a great hiding spot! They'd never find me! And they didn't. It was an hour or more when I finally crawled out from under the bed where I had hidden on top of a cedar chest, smashed up against the underside of the box springs. I had fallen asleep waiting for It to find me. But It got tired of looking, and when called to supper, she joined the family at the table for the evening meal. "Oh, Qené will get tired of hiding and come into dinner when she sees we're eating without her," they said. Only I didn't. I was fast asleep and only woke when one of the youngsters bounced on the bed and scared me out of my hiding place.

Cranky. I was cranky and whining. Whining, they thought, because I had just woken up and missed dinner. Whining, I thought, because no one loved me enough to miss me at the dinner table or to continue looking until I was found … safe and sound. For all they knew I could have been lost, not hiding … stolen away, not asleep under the bed on top of the cedar chest. They should have kept looking, but they didn't.

Yes, I've spent a lot of time hiding. The *Merriam-Webster Dictionary* has at least four different definitions of the word *hide*.[6] One is "to put out of sight: secrete; to conceal for shelter or protection." Well, that pretty much describes the cedar chest ordeal, don't you agree?

A second definition is "to keep secret; to hide the truth." I've always been good at keeping secrets. You can tell me anything, and it will never be told. Now, my daughter is another story. She's always believed that it's okay to tell a secret as long as you whisper … shhhhh. But some of my secrets can never be told, even in the quietest, gentlest breath of a whisper. There are no words to be uttered, no sounds to be made, no sense to be understood of all that must remain unknown. The secrets will be kept. I have much to hide.

"To screen from or as if from view; obscure" is another definition of the word *hide*. I laugh when I think of all the things I have hidden behind, trying to keep from being seen by something or someone. I would hide under the covers at night to escape being seen by the caged cardboard lion hanging on my wall. I would hide between my mother's legs to escape the wrath of my father. I would hide in my grandmother's lap, running from the taunts and teasing of my brother and sisters. I would hide behind long bangs combed low over my eyes to escape the look of boys I liked but was too shy to speak to. I would hide behind hats, long sleeves, baggy pants, and shoes, embarrassed by blemishes and pounds of flesh that really weren't there and could only be seen by me—thinking that there was nothing attractive enough in me to seen by others. So I hid using anything and everything to block the view of … me.

31

To hide is "to turn (the eyes or face) away in shame or anger." I turn away to hide my shyness, my embarrassment, my sorrow, my lack of self-esteem, my depression, my ugliness, my loneliness, my anger, my disappointment, my tears. I turn away so that I don't have to see the truth when it's too painful for me to bear.

Yes, I've done a lot of hiding in my lifetime, but several years ago I finally found a wonderful hiding place. I'll never look for another one because it's the best hiding place of all. Hidden with Christ in God! Imagine that! With Christ in God! I am hidden with Christ in God, and there's not a safer place to be.

Won't you join me? It's always more fun to hide with a friend.

"For [as far as this world is concerned] you have died, and your [new, real] life is hidden with Christ in God" (Colossians 3:3 AMPC).

Out, In, Down, and Up

O, Lord! I cry out! I cry out—searching the depths of Your heart for mercy and grace. Deep calls unto deep as my voice rises to the heavens waiting for You to hear and answer. My cry escapes polluted lips, begging to be cleansed by You. O, Lord! I cry out—knowing not where else to turn but to You. You alone are my Maker, my judge, my Redeemer, and Savior. Have mercy on me O, Lord—for I cry out to You!

O, Lord! I breathe in! I breathe in the grace and peace I have from knowing You. You fill my soul with the abundance of Your love, and I long for the understanding of the depth, height, and width of it. It covers and fills me O, Lord, and I breathe in freedom, breaking the yoke of my bondage to sin. O, Lord—I breathe in Your grace and peace.

O, Lord! I pray down! I pray down the strength of Your Spirit asking for Your favor to fall on me like rain. My hands hang down and my knees are feeble as I walk through this world alone, but Your strong arms lift me high above the fray and separates me from the cares of this world. Your strength becomes mine as I pray down, O, Lord, and I am filled with a power that is not my own. O, Lord—I pray down the favor of Your blessing.

O, Lord! I look up—You are my shield and the lifter of my head! The world would seek to bury me, to blind me with its glitz and glamor.

But You, O, Lord, draw my gaze up to Yours, the only treasure I seek is You. I search the skies endlessly expecting Your appearance. I wait and long for You to issue the call, "Come up here!" Please call us to come soon, Lord Jesus. The birth pains of this world are bearing down, and the clamor of groaning voices seeks to drown You out as You speak and call my name. O, Lord, as You lift my head—I look up to catch a vision of You.

"And when these things begin to come to pass, then look up, and lift up your heads; for your redemption draweth nigh" (Luke 21:28).

The One Who Keeps Us

If not for the Lord, we would surely have despaired and fainted in the way today. He alone is the reason we had strength, and a good measure of grace, when we were weak and overcome with our failings. We said, "I can't!" and He said, "I can!" Then through His great and Holy Spirit, He soaked us in His mercy, surrounded us with His strong arm, and lifted us high above the fray to that blessed place of His presence. For a moment, we wept and sighed. For a moment, we hid ourselves in Him.

Ah, yes! If not for the Lord, we would surely have sinned at every turn today, falling in the way of every temptation and snare, daring not to believe that He could save the likes of us—even from ourselves. But He provided a way out for us, a back door, a new avenue of courage, a measure of faith. Oh, the way was straight, and the way was narrow, but His yoke was easy, and His burden was light, and if not for the depth of His love, we surely would have turned our backs on Him today. But we love Him because He first loved us, and when He pulled us back from the brink of disaster, we saw the nail prints in His hands, that place where our names have been engraved.

He kept us! He whispered, "This is the way. I am the way." With beckoning hand high in the air, He declared, "Follow me!" And away we went on that straight and narrow, following hard after Him with heart pounding and lungs panting.

Ah, yes! If not for the Lord, none of it surely would have mattered today. But as it was, because of Him, it all mattered. Because of Him, it was all victory; it was all love. And so it is that at the end of this day we are able to bow in humble adoration for the one who keeps us, the one who blesses us—saves us. Surely when the morrow comes, His rest will have become our rest—we'll have His strength and a good measure of His grace for yet another day.

"Jesus saith unto him, I am the way, the truth, and the life: no man cometh unto the Father, but by me" (John 14:6).

Let Her Sing!

One of the things I love best about attending a small country church is that we sing the old hymns. Oh, now, I know that we don't sing them well, but we sing them with glad hearts and toes tapping to keep the beat. I'm not much of a vocalist, but no one enjoys singing more than I do! Occasionally, you might see me snickering and trying to remain calm and composed while singing in church. More often than not it's because my scratchy old lady throat barks out a yodel, and I can't hide how hysterically funny I think that is!

This past Sunday we sang a song that brought back a flash of memory ...

Many years ago—if it was five, it was fifty and five years ago—my mother was swinging on the porch with us children—me, my older sister, René, my younger sister, Tish, and our new baby brother, Jay-Jay. It was a happy night, and we were singing, laughing, and having fun. I was so happy, and I just couldn't quit. I sang every song I knew, and a few I didn't! I was pickin' up pawpaws with Perry Como, catching falling stars and putting them in my pocket, and always, always counting the verses about the little rabbit who ain't got no tail at all. Ha! What a fun time I was having. On and on I went ...

Well, you know how sisters are! And mine just weren't feeling it! Finally, unable to endure one more verse, they both cried out, "Momma! Momma! Please! Make her stop! Make her stop!" I remember my mother laughing, and she said, "Oh, girls! She's so happy. Let her sing!" And sing I did, on and on into the summer night air.

It was but a day or two later, surely no more than twenty and one years, that I sat with my children in a hot car on a summer afternoon, waiting for their dad to walk out of the milk plant and come home with us for his lunch. We were hot, sure enough, but we enjoyed the day while passing the time singing every song we knew and a few we didn't. Little three-year-old Noni was so happy, just singing her heart out! The boys had long since tired, but still, she sang on and on making her way through the Baptist hymnal the best she could remember. "Victory in Jesus"; "Holy, Holy, Holy!"; "There Is Power in the Blood"; and finally her favorite, "Are You Washed in the Blood?" She was happy, she was singing, and she just couldn't quit …

"Mommy, Mommy! Please, Mommy, make her stop! We can't stand it anymore. Please, oh, please!" The boys, P. J. and Woodi, cried in unison. With a quick flash of memory back to the days before, I said, "Oh, boys! She is so happy! Let her sing!" And sing, she did! "Are you washed in the blood of the Lamb … are your garments spotless … are they white as snow … are you washed in the Blood of the Lamb?"[7]

Beloved, is someone trying to stop you from singing your happy tune? Regardless of who, or what, or why, the heavens are ringing out, "Let her sing!"

Sing on, my friends. Someone needs to hear your song!

"I will sing unto the LORD as long as I live; I will sing praise to my God while I have my being" (Psalm 104:33).

The Long Walk Home

My legs were short. My arms were full. My shoes were untied. And everyone was about a block ahead of me.

"Hey, wait up!" I yelled. "Wait for me!"

Their legs ran even faster, racing to get home. I tripped on my shoelace and dropped my books. Tired and exasperated, I stopped and plopped down on the roadway, gathering my skirt around me and tying my shoelaces the best I could. They were tattered and torn, knotted together in a quick-fix sort of way. Beyond repair, I tossed them aside and began stacking my books one on top of another, ready to make my way home and face the music.

"What took you so long, Slowpoke?" they would chant.

Looking down the road, I could see that they were far away by now and out of earshot to my yell for help. That's the way it always was. No matter how much I hurried, everyone was always way ahead of me. I never had a chance, really. They were usually halfway home before I even got started. My pleas for them to wait up would only make them run faster. So I often walked the long road home alone, tears mixing with the dust on my cheeks, making little mud pies as they dried on my face.

Sometimes, I still feel like that exasperated seven-year-old, holding my dusty books as I saunter off toward home. Everyone else has run on ahead of me and left me to carry the books and tend to my shoelaces. The road home is dry and dusty and long. I am weary, my steps are slow, and there are many stops on the way to tie my shoes and toss away the broken laces that trip me up.

Calls to "Wait up! Wait for me!" fall from my lips and float away in the wind. My tears dry on my face as I struggle on the way.

In the distance, I see a lone figure. Curious, I pick up my step, and I faintly hear a familiar voice.

"Come! Come, Qenè, and follow Me!"

He smiles, waves, and urges me on. Suddenly my load isn't heavy, the road isn't lonely, and the things that would trip me up are cast away out of the path of my running feet.

"I'm coming!" I yell. "I'm coming!"

And I run. I run like the wind, invigorated by the sound of His voice. Smiling and waving, He bids me on. I feel His Spirit rise within me as He bears my load. He walks the long, dusty road with me and then He pauses at the gate to welcome me home.

> "Hast thou not known? Hast thou not heard, that the everlasting God, the LORD, the Creator of the ends of the earth, fainteth not, neither is weary? There is no searching of his understanding. He giveth power to the faint; and to them that have no might he increaseth strength. Even the youths shall faint and be weary, and the young men shall utterly fall: But they that wait

upon the LORD shall renew their strength; they shall mount up with wings as eagles; they shall run, and not be weary, and they shall walk, and not faint" (Isaiah 40:28–31).

Who Would Love Us?

Each day the Lord pours His unfailing love upon us, and through each night we sing His songs, praying to God who gives us life. Friends, let's put our hope in Him! He is our sanctuary, our stronghold, the light of our lives. Where could we go if not to Him? Who would love us if He did not?

Ah, but He does love us—with an everlasting love, He loves us! We can have confidence in Him because He is our confidence! We can declare, "Here I am, Lord—the one that You love! Send out Your light and truth to guide me. Lead me to Your holy mountain, to the place where You live. I will come to You, the source of all my joy. I will lift up holy hands to praise You."

He is our refuge and our strength! When I'm in trouble? He's always ready to help me! Let's be still in His presence, soaking up His peace so that we will have no fear. Let us meditate on His unfailing love. When we awaken in the night, let praise pass our lips before our feet hit the floor. Let our hearts be glad in the assurance of His watchful care. He is our God forever and ever. He will guide us until we die, and then we will be with Him forevermore. And so it will be.

Beloved, I am praying for God's blessings of good health and rest as we tuck our tired old bones in bed for the night. May we be refreshed with His love! He is sitting at the right hand of God, ever interceding for us. We can rest well in that!

"There I will go to the altar of God, to God—the source of all my joy. I will praise you with my harp, O God, my God!" (Psalm 43:4 NLT).

"Thou wilt shew me the path of life: in thy presence *is* fullness of joy; at thy right hand *there are* pleasures for evermore" (Psalm 16:11).

"Therefore he is able, once and forever, to save those who come to God through him. He lives forever to intercede with God on their behalf" (Hebrews 7:25 NLT).

Baseball and Roses

Just in case you were wondering, February 14, 1970, was on a Saturday. I was fifteen years old and spent the day outside playing baseball with my brother and sisters. I had a mean throwing arm, so I was pitching. I used to practice my pitch for hours, or at least until I ran out of sisters who would catch. We loved playing ball in the yard!

We hadn't been playing long when a florist van pulled in the driveway—a man walked across the yard and handed me a beautiful red rose. Thinking it could be for my sister René, I stopped to look at the card while holding my ball glove between my knees.

The card envelope was bright red and had type on every single inch of it! My eyes quickly scanned the card, and I realized that there were just three words typed over and over across the face of the envelope. But right there in the middle of the envelope was a word, a name that was different from all the other words. Every word was carefully typed on that red Valentine envelope.

It only took a split second for me to see that the name in the middle started with a Q, not an R!

Qené. The card said Qené! It said, *"I love you, I love you, I love you, Qené; I love you, I love you ..."* Those three words completely covered the card!

With a huge smile on my face, and a squeal of delight that echoed through the city streets of Neosho - I grabbed my glove, the rose vase, and card, and I ran. Leaving my brother, sisters and a few ghost runners holding the ball without a pitcher, I ran like a flash into the house to tell my mother.

"Momma, look! Look, it's for me! I got a rose for Valentine's Day!" And there I stood with my ball glove in one hand and a rose in the other as she laughed and rolled her eyes at her silly girl-child.

She said, "Okay, Qené! Which is it going to be? Will it be baseball or boys?"

Without missing a beat, I answered, "Pat! Momma, it's going to be Pat!"

And so it was. And so it is. We are living happily ever after! Amen!

"...I found him whom my soul loveth: I held him, and would not let him go..." (Song of Solomon 3:4).

A Tale of Great Woe

The day had arrived. It was a day that most teenagers look forward to, but one which I thoroughly feared and dreaded. I had put it off for many weeks, hoping that with each passing day I would grow more confident and more at ease with the whole process. But that was never going to happen, and it was with trembling hands, weak knees, and tears wetting my lashes and cheeks that I arrived at the DMV to take my driver's license exam.

I had taken the written exam many months prior and was very excited to receive a perfect score. I had to guess on several of the answers, but the prayers of my friends from the Catholic high school I attended paid off. I prayed to every saint I could think of, and I passed the written exam to become the proud but apprehensive owner of a driver's permit.

Over the next several weeks, I filled as many hours as possible behind the wheel of my mother's 1968 green, wood-paneled Dodge station wagon. I drove the car, with my mom or big sister in tow, at every opportunity.

Any time an errand needed to be run, I was there with keys in hand and my permit safely tucked away in my hip pocket, ready to make the trip through the busy streets of our town. I was a nervous wreck each time I got behind the wheel and prayed that no one would see the tremor in my hands, nor the sweat of my brow, as I slowly and painstakingly pulled out of the driveway.

I must say that my nervousness was most likely the result of my very first driving experience. A year prior, as a sophomore in high school, I was required to take a driver's class. My first day out on the road was not a great experience for me. I am sure the driving instructor and my classmates riding in the backseat would agree. In fact, I left class that day swearing to never get in another car in my life. I was embarrassed by my tears that day, but I was even more embarrassed by the little ride I took them on—through a yard and around all the trees and bushes of a house on Oak Ridge Drive. Every time I touched the steering wheel or gas pedal, the car would seem to leap and spin out of control. As the car approached bushes and trees, the instructor would quickly put on his brake, which brought us to an abrupt stop. We made a quick tour of the yard leaping and bucking like a wild animal as the instructor took his turn on the brake, and I took my turn on the gas pedal. All the while, a horrified little lady stood on the porch in her housecoat with a tea towel clutched tightly to her mouth watching the whole affair. I was mortified.

As I finally gained control of the wheel and headed in the direction of the street, the instructor turned to survey the yard to make sure I had caused no damage to the any of the carefully planted bushes and plants. With a wave of his hand to the petrified woman, I drove reluctantly down the street. I was painfully aware that the student driver sign on the back of the car didn't even begin to describe my inexperience.

Yes, that memory was in my mind every time I got behind the wheel. As I sat in the license bureau awaiting my turn for the driving test, I tried to concentrate on counting the tile squares on the floor, pausing at each one to say a Hail Mary and beg the Lord for mercy and grace.

Finally, my name was called. The police officer seemed so gruff and unwelcoming. I gave him a weak smile as we climbed into the car, hoping that he would return my gesture of friendliness. He was obviously cranky, and I felt very uneasy. I was so intimidated by him—and rightly so, it would seem. I was very nervous about driving in this very busy part of town on a day that had been filled with light rain. Yes, the odds were definitely stacked against me.

On the verge of tears, not to mention a possible nervous breakdown, my heart was racing, my hands were shaking, and my knees were knocking as I turned the key in the ignition. The prayer on my lips was, "Please, Mother of God, don't let me drive through anyone's yard today."

I was parallel parked on a busy business street. As the light rain continued, I checked my mirrors, looked behind me, and mentally made the sign of the cross. I followed the policeman's directions, and as I pulled into the lane of traffic, the worst possible thing that could have happened did happen—I hit a moving vehicle.

The test was over before it even began. I dissolved into a bundle of nerves and tears. The gruff policeman said through clenched teeth, "Do you think you can back it up next to the curb?" With trembling hands, I did the best I could and sat waiting for the policeman to get information from the nice little gentleman who timed his right turn just as I was pulling away from the corner.

"Well, Missy, you don't pass when you hit a moving vehicle." We exited the car and went back into the license bureau. My older sister, René, looked up and was surprised to see us so soon. My tears told her that I didn't pass, and the pink ticket told her I was in trouble. Big trouble.

René drove me to the hospital where my mother worked. It was supposed to have been a fun trip in to see her to show off my new driver's license. But instead, I ran down the hall with tears streaming down my face. She hugged me and said, "Oh, honey, you flunked your test." Between sobs, I declared, "Oh, Mother, I wrecked your car."

About a week later, I had to appear before the juvenile judge in our county courthouse. He was as stern as the policeman had been, and he made me go through the whole story of what had happened. I felt like a criminal—a wolf dressed up in sheep's clothing of a parochial school uniform. His lecture made it sound like I was a rebellious teenager who needed a good spanking. The last words he said to me before I left the room were, "I don't ever want to see you in here again!" I was humiliated.

I waited about a year before I was ready to take my test again. Our family priest drove me to a small nearby town to take the exam. He sat in the waiting room while I once again tried to prove that I was a competent driver worthy to be licensed. He said the rosary while I was driving, and we were both very relieved that this time I passed the test. I passed! Thank you, God!

About six months later my sister just younger than me wanted to take her driving test. I offered to go with her—and of course, she wanted to drive on her permit to practice on the way to the DMV. She was nervous. So was I. We both said our prayers on the way downtown.

I suggested she park in the back of the building where the parking was at an angle rather than parallel in the front as I had done. I didn't want her pulling out and hitting someone who was turning the corner and into her lane of traffic. Tish was grateful for the suggestion, and she circled the parking lot looking for a parking space. Finding one fairly close by, she pulled in between two parked cars. I can't begin to express my shock when she pulled in so close to the car on the right that she scraped the whole side of our car against it! It was so close that the door handles locked, one over the other. The sound of metal scraping metal is a terrible, terrible sound.

Looking up with shock and horror on our faces, we saw that the examination policeman was standing on the sidewalk right in front of us talking to the owner of the car. Could anything possibly be worse?

Hysterical tears were shed instantly, a ticket was written, and we never made it inside to inquire about the test. I drove her down to the hospital where my mother still worked. It was supposed to be an exciting visit. Mom expected her girls to run down the hospital halls waving a new driver's license as we approached her workstation. Instead, she was greeted by the sobs and tears of two teenaged daughters. "Oh, honey," she said, "You flunked your test." Finding air between her sobs my sister declared in a broken voice, "Oh, Mother, I wrecked your car."

Yes, the same scenario, the same judge, with the same warning not to ever darken his courtroom door again. I have a feeling that comment was directed toward my mother. It was to be several months before my sister even dared to take the test.

My boyfriend, Pat, came home on leave from Navy boot camp that fall, and one day while I was in play practice after school, he took my sister downtown to get her license.

It was a very uneventful afternoon. She passed.

My Song Is a New Song

Many years ago, my song was a flat, two-note dirge with no melody, no harmony, and no joyful chorus. There was no dance in my step, no lilt to my voice, no purpose for my song.

But one day I met Yeshua, the Savior. He took my cold, hard heart of stone and gave me a heart of flesh. He turned everything that was wrong into everything that was right. I no longer stumble my way through the obstacles of life. No, He is walking with me, carrying me along life's way on the straight and narrow, lifting me up with His strong arm.

The beautiful melody of my new song bounces against the walls of the universe. My heart is light, and there is a spring in my step and a twirl in my skirt as we dance to a new melodious song of joy and unfettered peace.

I rest in His arms when I grow weary. I rely on His confidence when I don't know the steps. He keeps me from falling when the tempo is too fast. My new song is praise flowing from my lips, gratitude filling my heart to overflowing. It is a glorious tune that I hum throughout the day and rest in through the night. Thank you, Lord Jesus!

Save the last dance for me, Yeshua. I feel the time drawing near. I hear the band warming up, and a chorus of hallelujah drifting through the clouds from heaven.

"But let all who take refuge in you rejoice; let them sing joyful praises forever. Spread your protection over them, that all who love your name may be filled with joy. For you bless the godly, O LORD; you surround them with your shield of love" (Psalm 5:11–12 NLT).

God Chose This One

If I close my eyes really tight and lift my face up to the sun, I can still remember how it was that day, all of some fifty-five years ago. I can feel the sun hot on my skin. I can smell the grass and flowering bushes where my sisters and I often hid under the blossoms to play house with our imaginary husbands and baby dolls. I can hear the breeze rustling through the full treetops, a bird whistling in the distance, and the sound of my bare feet pounding the pavement over and over again. Right foot, left foot, right foot, left foot, right foot. My breath is heavy in my chest as I jump; my curls are wet with sweat as I count and chant …

Gypsy, gypsy, please tell me,

What my fortune's going to be.

Rich man? Poor man? Beggar man? Thief?

Doctor? Lawyer? Indian chief?

Tinker? Tailor? Cowboy? Sailor?

Who will I marry? What will he be?

We will have to wait and see.

One … two … three …

Eight years old and jumping rope on the hot pavement, I had no idea what my future held other than a peanut butter and jelly sandwich for lunch. I couldn't look much beyond the current pages of the book I was reading or the branches of the next tree I would climb. At that moment, my future consisted of swimming lessons, fights with my sisters, summer afternoon naps and a baseball game with the neighbor boys, and ghost runners.

Who will I marry? What will he be?

We will have to wait and see …

I open my eyes now and turn from the sun. The heat felt good on my face for those few minutes and the memory of that day, so sweet. I look back over the years of my life, and through hindsight glasses I can see the hand of God molding me, shaping me, and turning life's direction in such a way as to bless me. The gypsy held no special fortune in her crystal ball, but God held me tightly in His hands and carved out a beautiful, wonderful life for me.

I turn to look at the man who sits beside me. Strong and upright he sits in our pew; handsome and confident in his blue suit of clothes with his Bible held tightly under his arm. I look under my lashes to see his tired eyes, the deep furrows in his face, and the gray hair that silently speaks of long nights in prayer. I stroke the hands of a sailor who sailed the seas, the hands of a father who raised three children, and the hands of a preacher man who turns the pages to rightly divide the Word of truth. I look deep into his hazel eyes. The playful boy I once knew is still there, and I see a hint of his smile as he rises to the pulpit and as I silently count and chant …

Who will I marry? What will he be?

God chose this one just for me …

"There be three things which are too wonderful for me, yea, four which I know not: The way of an eagle in the air; the way of a serpent upon a rock; the way of a ship in the midst of the sea; and the way of a man with a maid" (Proverbs 30:18–19).

A Priceless Gift

He wanted a Christmas tree. I wanted a nativity.

The year was 1973, and it was our first Christmas together in our home, located in Chula Vista, California. He spent most of that year on a tour of duty in Vietnam sweeping the harbor for mines. We were away from family, we were away from friends, but it was home because we were finally together. I was content with that.

After much discussion and counting of coins, the Christmas tree won out. Not because he was stronger, or selfish, or a slick talker. No, the tree won because it was cheaper than the nativity, and we were poor folk living on the wages of a United States Navy sailor. I didn't mind. I was just glad to be with him, and once the tree was set and a few homemade decorations placed in the branches, I forgot all about the nativity ... almost.

One sunny afternoon, on a warm day in mid-December, my groom arrived home from duty with a smile on his face and his hands behind his back. We teasingly played coy guessing games, I chased him around the room, and finally when flirting and sweet talk didn't work, he slowly brought his hands around for my eyes to see.

As he opened his fingers, I saw the faint colors of pink, blue, and gold. I couldn't believe it as he held open his cupped hands and revealed the daintiest, most perfect little nativity that I had ever seen! The pieces were no more than three inches tall, but their shape and color were perfect in every way. There sat beautiful mother Mary, gazing lovingly at her baby. Proud Joseph, staff in hand, stood at her side beholding the beloved Christ child. And there in a little manger, perfect and precious, was the Son of God, Son of Man, Yeshua, our Jesus.

I cried with joy that day! And all these years later, I still remember the excitement of that moment. My shrieks of glee filled the room as I begged to know how he came to own it—to give it. He proudly shared the story of how he saw it in the ship's store window as a decoration for Christmas. The minute he saw it, he knew he had to have it. It was only after much talking and convincing that he was able to purchase it for me, his bride. The purchase took every penny of the change he had in his pocket, but at the time, the price of two dollars seemed small for such a treasure that was so valued, so desired, so loved.

For many years that little nativity was the only one I owned. I now own more than forty sets, big and little, plain and beautiful. But that little nativity, that priceless gift from my beloved Pat, is my favorite of them all.

Receiving this priceless gift and claiming it as my own reminds me of the priceless and perfect gift given to us by our heavenly Father. It is unlike any gift that has ever been given or received. It is truly a gift beyond compare.

"But as many as received him, to them gave he power to become the sons of God, even to them that believe on his name: Which were born, not of blood, nor of the will of the flesh, nor of the will of man, but of God. And the Word was made flesh, and dwelt among us, (and we beheld his glory, the glory as of the only-begotten of the Father,) full of grace and truth" (John 1:12–14).

The Father gave me Jesus and I received Him. Have you?

"And so it was, that, while they were there, the days were accomplished that she should be delivered. And she brought forth her firstborn son, and wrapped him in swaddling clothes, and laid him in a manger; because there was no room for them in the inn.

And there were in the same country shepherds abiding in the field, keeping watch over their flock by night. And, lo, the angel of the Lord came upon them, and the glory of the Lord shone round about them: and they were sore afraid. And the angel said unto them, Fear not: for, behold, I bring you good tidings of great joy, which shall be to all people. For unto you is born this day in the city of David a Savior, which is Christ the Lord. And this shall be a sign unto you; Ye shall find the babe wrapped in swaddling clothes, lying in a manger.

And suddenly there was with the angel a multitude of the heavenly host praising God, and saying, Glory to God in the highest, and on earth peace, good will toward men." (Luke 2:6–14)

It's All in a Name

Many years ago, early in our marriage, my Pat and I were out with a few friends having dinner. Somehow our conversation turned to love names—you know, the nicknames that couples commonly give to one another? Some of the names were hilariously funny, like Little Love Muffin, Papa Bear, Baby Cakes. The list went on and on, and we laughed until we were silly! But, suddenly the laughter quieted, and someone asked me, "How about it, Qené? What love name does Pat have for you?"

I was silent for a moment, and I was kind of embarrassed to admit it, but at that time Pat never called me anything but my given name. No Sweetie-Peetie, no Sugar-Booger, no Hunny Bunches for me. No love name. Just my name. Just Qené.

As soon as I said it, all eyes were on Pat! "What? What's wrong with you? No nickname for your little woman?"

How weird that seemed in the middle of this funny conversation with people who had several love names for one another. But Pat had none for me.

Then he said it. "Her name is so beautiful to me! Why would I want to call her anything else?" Now, in the silence at that table, that was definitely the right thing to say! Oh, my! Who could feel badly about that? Not me! And since that evening I have always loved to hear my Pat say my name!

Now, I tell you that little story to tell you this—while we love the name of our Savior, Jesus, the sweetest name I know, the name that makes tears puddle in the corner of my eyes is the name Mary called her little baby boy: Yeshua. Yeshua is the name the makes me whisper, "Holy!" Yeshua is the name I sing silently in my heart. Yeshua is the love name of my Savior, my Lord, and my friend. Yeshua, son of God, Son of Man. A name so sweet, so powerful, that angels worship and demons tremble! Yeshua. Oh, how I love His name!

It's been about forty-four years since that little happening in a San Diego restaurant, and you will be glad to know that in all this time Pat finally does have a few little love names that he calls me. But my favorite will always be Qené because it is so beautiful to my beloved Pat.

"And she shall bring forth a Son, and she shall call his name Yeshua, for he shall save his people from their sins" (Matthew 12:1 Aramaic Bible in Plain English).

And So It Is

Sitting side by side on the couch, they said their morning prayers. At the last "Amen," he turned slightly to kiss her full on the mouth.

"That's getting harder to do," he said. "We don't bend and move quite as easily as we used to."

"I know," she replied. "We are getting old."

"Yes, it's happening just as we planned," he declared. "We are growing old together."

And so it is.

"Let thy fountain be blessed, and rejoice with the wife of thy youth" (Proverbs 5:18).

Birds of a Feather

When I was twenty-six years old, I came to the truth that I could no longer rely on the faith of my parents or the doctrines of my church to claim salvation for me. It was a personal choice I had to make for myself. So, during a very difficult year emotionally, physically, and spiritually, I began following hard after God, and I made a personal profession of my faith in Christ. One of the first things I did on my journey of faith was to enroll in a Bible class I heard about through a local church. The class was on Saturday mornings at 6:00 a.m. at a pastor's home.

My three children were very young, and I couldn't take them with me. My husband worked on Saturdays, so for me to attend this Bible study was a really big deal. I had to find a babysitter that would come to my home while my children were still (hopefully) asleep. I had to pay a sitter with money we didn't have, and as I soon discovered after I paid the fee for the Bible study, the class was made up of only pastors and their spouses. I was way out of my league and didn't have a clue! All I knew for certain was that I had a brand-new Bible and I had absolutely no idea how to read it. However, my desire to learn was bigger than my intimidation, and I wasn't going to let anything stop me from going to this study!

One Saturday, I was running late in getting to the class. My house had to be clean and breakfast ready before I was comfortable in having a babysitter over. This was a huge task for me! But I came flying into Bible study on the seat of my pants, apologizing for being late, with my Bible, books, and purse spilling into the room with me. Oh, I was just sure that those pastors would rather I stayed home.

But L. D. Sowder, one of my favorite pastors of all time, greeted me with this: "Oh, Qené! We are so delighted you are here! We were afraid you'd given up on us. It's such a pleasure to see you flying through the door with your feathers all aflutter after taking care of your little chicks so you could be here to study with us. You add a lot of excitement and fun to this room of old, sour pastors." What a blessing their welcoming spirit was to me!

All these years later, I am so thankful for the investment those pastors made in my life! And it wasn't long after that little event happened that I came across this verse:

> "Don't be concerned about the outward beauty of fancy hairstyles, expensive jewelry, or beautiful clothes. You should clothe yourselves instead with the beauty that comes from within, the unfading beauty of a gentle and quiet spirit, which is so precious to God. This is how the holy women of old made themselves beautiful. They put their trust in God and accepted the authority of their husbands (1 Peter 3:3–5 NLT).

I determined that if it was precious to God, then that's what I wanted my life to be. I didn't want my feathers fluttering and flying about, causing a stir everywhere I went. I wanted a spirit that was gentle and quiet. I wanted to be a holy woman of old!

Now, the fact that I'm still studying that word in 1 Peter should tell you that I haven't yet acquired that gentleness and quietness of spirit. I have a long, long way to go before I am a holy woman of old. Oh, goodness, my feathers flutter about enough that no one would ever doubt that!

But, my heart is set on it. And even though I still flutter and sputter, I am learning to keep my peace and walk with a gentle and quiet spirit, which is so pleasing to God.

At the end of the day, when all is said and done, I close my eyes in quiet rest, gently whispering the name of our Savior, Yeshua, because I know that He is the one who brings me true peace. He will ever be my Prince of Peace, the one who calms my heart, and the one who smooths my feathers.

Searching for Truth

I open the cover and turn the pages of Your Word, searching for a bit of truth this morning, Lord. Where will I find that which speaks to my life if not but in the whole of it? I need Your truth to fill all those broken places in my heart, those spaces that harbor sin and ugliness. Spaces that I have long forgotten or perhaps have intentionally deserted and ignored.

What truth will I find in Your Word today, Lord, which You prepared to change me even before the foundations of the world were created? My eyes cannot but look therein without the conviction of Your Spirit and Your truth speaking to my darkness, commanding it to flee.

What transgressions will Your blood have to cover today, O Savior? What inadequacies will Your strong Spirit have to heal and bind up as a buckler of truth and grace? What lie will You have to cast out in the name of truth and holiness?

I dread the pain of Your Word piercing my flesh, dividing asunder my spirit and soul, cutting through bone to separate joint and marrow, and even discerning my thoughts and the intents of my heart. It is a surgery that must be done, and my dread turns to hope and hope to joy as I experience the life-changing power of Your Word in me.

"Thou art near, O LORD; and all thy commandments are truth" (Psalm 119:151).

"For the Word that God speaks is alive and full of power [making it active, operative, energizing, and effective]; it is sharper than any two-edged sword, penetrating to the dividing line of the breath of life (soul) and [the immortal] spirit, and of joints and marrow [of the deepest parts of our nature], exposing and sifting and analyzing and judging the very thoughts and purposes of the heart" (Hebrews 4:12 AMPC).

My Life in the Fishbowl

The fishbowl I look into is so calm and serene. It holds a certain fascination for me. I watch the fish who live there, sometimes floating aimlessly, enjoying their calm waters. Sometimes, they are so busy moving rocks, digging pathways, and making this bowl their home. Sometimes, they are streaks in the water, chasing one another with a speed that is awesome to behold in such a small place! But often, I have to look closely to find them. It's as if they departed to a secret place to be alone hiding in the corner, perhaps asleep, or just escaping my watchful eye. Sometimes, as I sit in my chair beside their home, I find them watching *me* closely. Any movement on my part causes a swift retreat behind the plastic shrubs and pet rocks that my children have used to decorate this water mansion.

At meal times when I approach their doorway, they rise to greet me, anxious for the food they know I bring. It always pleases me when they linger after they have received their sprinkling. There is an unspoken communication of gratitude as they nibble at my finger in the water and then quickly swim off to eat their powdered treasure. It's always the same treasure, never changing. But they are thankful just the same, and I am grateful for the time they allow me to be a visitor in their home, soaking up their serenity and marveling at their gracefulness. They are at peace with the world, and their offering is given in silence.

Recently I read a newsletter for pastors' wives. It was written by pastors' wives and of course talked about life at home with the pastor. Several women wrote about their lives in the fishbowl of the ministry, proclaiming both the blessing and the curse that fills their fishbowl home. I understood every word. I identified with every blessing ... every curse. And I agreed with every conclusion, that the blessings that are abundant and rich far outweigh the curse. The curse is often painful and unexpected, but it passes quickly and is usually followed by a blessing indescribable.

Sometimes, when people look into my fishbowl home, I wonder what they are seeing. What are they looking for? Do they go away satisfied?

Ours is a busy little fishbowl with people coming and going and making themselves at home. This is where life happens for this preacher's family. This is where we truly live out that which is within us. Sometimes life is quiet and serene. We seem to float from one activity to the next, aware of one another's needs and soaking up the peacefulness to save for a more harried and hurried future. And that time will come. It always comes! Our life is often fast and hectic, leaving a stir of dust in the wake, turning our little fishbowl into a dust bowl where tempers are short, feelings get hurt, and everyone is in need of a hug.

I saw a wonderful visual illustration about life in the fishbowl. The bowl was a blender, the blender was plugged in, and the poor little fish with big eyes was waiting for his head to spin! He was saying, "And you think you're stressed out!" We have our days like that; days where we are crazy with fear that someone will push our buttons and things in the fishbowl will never be the same. God's Word is such a comfort during those times. We look up to Jesus knowing and believing that "thou wilt keep him in perfect peace whose mind is stayed on Thee ..." (Isaiah 26:3). And, we wait for the calm and peaceful living water to flood our souls and fill our bowl.

Often, when we peer out the windows of our home, we find that those we've been called to minister to are peering back at us. It is tempting to retreat and hide because it's so easy to doubt our calling into this fishbowl called ministry. We do so want to make a difference! But often we are troubled when we realize that we've made no difference at all.

The view is clear from our bowl. We look out to see grace in action, and we can't believe our good fortune in getting to watch God close at hand, working in lives, touching hearts, and blessing His people. Those are the times that make us rejoice! Those are the times of refreshing! And we are grateful for the blessing, soaking up His serenity, marveling at His gracefulness. We are at peace with God, and our offering of praise is given with love.

Is It for Me? Or Is It for You?

Sometimes I save copies of little notes that I write to other people and I give them to myself. Oh, I know how silly it may sound, but when I find myself in the same circumstance, many times those little notes are what pull me through.

Before I write a note of encouragement to someone, I pray and ask God for direction and wisdom to speak into this life of someone I know and love who is hurting. Sometimes, the Lord gives me a word of wisdom for that person—and then months, weeks, or years later, He will give me the same bit of wisdom to give to myself. It's really not so strange—the scriptures tell us that King David, during the most troubled time of his life, encouraged himself in the Lord. This is much the same thing, as many of the things I write come directly from scripture. They are truly His words and not mine. I imagine David asked himself the same question I've heard many others ask, including myself: Who is going to encourage the encourager? I learned a long time ago that if I don't do it, nobody will. Perhaps that's why King David learned to encourage himself in the Lord. It is a faith builder when you have to do it yourself.

I want to share a message with you that I sent to a pastor's wife years ago. She was suffering from a church's mistreatment of her husband when he was going through a mental health issue. It was painful. The evil one's breath was hot on her neck with accusations. He left her believing that she was totally worthless to the kingdom of God, that there was nothing further the Lord would ask her family to do in His name. Her husband was too sick to give her much encouragement or to help his family find their way out of this deep, black hole of depression that resulted from their mistreatment.

Shortly after I sent this note to her, I went through a terrible time of trial! Many nights I found myself reading and rereading this just to get some comfort from these words that came from directly from His heart to mine. My prayer is that you would find one or two words or phrases that speak to what you are going through. Words that you can chew as cud and pull out time and time again to ruminate on them. They might be words that will pull you through.

> Beloved, even in the middle of your trials, the loneliness, and fear, our Lord is making you into a beautiful vessel fit for His use. You can't judge your worthiness to minister by anyone's esteem to value you, even those of us who love you dearly and feel your pain as if it were our own.

> Only God can look at your fragile heart and declare it strong enough to serve and bring glory to His Name. Only God will know when the kiln of your tribulation has refined you in the fire, making you strong enough to bear the next area of ministry that He assigns to you.

> But in the meantime, the Lord beacons you to come to Him! You are burdened and heavy laden. Oh, how He longs to give you rest. Rest from your labor, rest from your care, rest from the gossip and hurtful comments, rest from the critical eye, rest from yourself and trying to figure it all out, rest from your fear, shame, and low self-esteem.

He, the one who created the universe, has esteemed you highly. The blood of His Son has soaked you through and through. It has covered your sin and filled your heart. It is what makes your fragile heart strong enough that it will not break, even though Satan has tossed you about and declared you unfit. Satan has desired to sift you like wheat, but *He*, our Savior Himself, has prayed for you that your faith may not fail.

Jesus longs to give you His burden. It is easy. It is light. It is your time to learn from Him and wait upon Him. You don't have to figure it all out, because He is busy working behind the scenes, and your eye hath not seen, nor has your ear heard, and your heart cannot possibly imagine all that He has prepared for you! He is able to do superabundantly more that you can hope for, pray for, long for or dream for. And He's not just going to do it for you—but also for your family so that their faith will be strong and so that in their unbelief they will believe. He can also make them into beautiful vessels fit for His use. He is begging you, "Beloved, learn to wait on me."

Believe me when I tell you that this trial is not for you. It is for us. Because one day you will turn to us in our despair and tribulation and you will strengthen us, your sisters.

Let Him envelop you in His grace and tuck you in tight with His love. Rest well, rest in Him. You are loved with the everlasting love of our Savior, Yeshua.

Please, consider these scriptures:

1 Samuel 30:6
Hebrews 13:17
1 Peter 5:8
Psalm 1:2
Psalm 19:14
Isaiah 26:3–4
Matthew 11:28–30
Mark 9:24
Psalm 46:10
Luke 22:31–32

Putting My Best Foot Forward

Today was a special day. It was my husband's first day as the new pastor of a lovely little church in rural Missouri.

They were very excited. They've been without a pastor for almost a year and were about to give up all hope of finding the one God had chosen for them.

We were very excited. For the past year, we've been without a church to call our own and have been filling the pulpits of several different churches in our corner of the state each Sunday. We were about to give up all hope of finding the church family God had chosen for us.

So today was a special day, but it was a typically busy Sunday morning, and as my habit has been of late, I was running behind and throwing on clothes and shoes as we raced out the door for our forty-five minute drive to church. It wouldn't be good to be late the first official Sunday as pastor.

We arrived just in time for me to visit the ladies room before the church service started. Glancing down as I turned around to flush, I realized that I was wearing two different shoes—a heel and a flat! I was so startled by my hasty choice of footwear that I let out a little scream and scared the lady in the stall next to me. A few minutes later, as other women came in to hear what the commotion was about, they found us hugging one another and laughing hysterically—we could barely stand up.

I told her that I had another pair of shoes at home just like these. Hopefully, I won't wear them next Sunday.

"A merry heart doeth good like a medicine: but a broken spirit drieth the bones" (Proverbs 17:22).

"What is that in your mouth?" Every mother has asked that dreaded question at one time or another.

Sometimes it's asked as a child's lips are turning blue with panic written across his face and tears rolling down his cheeks.

Sometimes it's asked as the child runs around to the back of the couch, trying to hide red lips and a mouthful of makeup or candy.

Sometimes, it's asked as a mother becomes aware of a chewing mouth trying to soften up rotten old gum that was stuck under the table at McDonald's. It always amazes me when that is more tempting than a Happy Meal! There's just something about that beloved chew that kids love regardless of who chewed it first.

"What is that in your mouth?" I asked as my friend and I sat watching our young children play. Two-year-old Woodi chose to stay close to the patio playing with trucks and cars, petting the dog, and making a little city with sticks and gravel. As I watched him play, I noticed he had a rather large object in his mouth and that prompted my curtness as I repeated, "Woodi, what is that in your mouth?"

Glancing up from his play, he noted that my feet were no longer resting in a chair but had suddenly taken the stance of stand-and-run. He moved quickly and stood and ran with his fat little hand clasped tightly over his mouth. I chased him around the backyard, and he managed to escape my grasp several times as I slid in the grass. It was perfect timing for him, and he took that opportunity to hide under the table using aluminum legs as a shield from the arms that were trying to grab him.

He knew what was coming. The finger sweep. And he hated it. He would often stamp his foot, shake his finger, and exclaim in his own Dutchy language, "You no put your feeners in my mouf no more."

I was finally able to grab him by the leg and pull him to safety, where I promptly forced my finger into his mouth exclaiming once again, "What is that in your mouth?"

My finger poked through clenched teeth and gums trying to find the surely dangerous item. Neither my friend nor I were prepared for what we saw. She, who had been laughing at the chase and capture of this two-year-old, was now gawking with opened mouth and bugged eyes. "What is that in his mouth?" she questioned.

The first inspection revealed a rather large, gray mass that looked a lot like the aforementioned chewy treat. Close inspection revealed something else that made us both wretch and gag, during which Woodi once again used that opportunity to stand and run, hoping to escape a swat or scolding for putting the "what is that" in his mouth.

It was several seconds before I could compose my gagging mouth to choke out the words, "It's a dog tick!" The declaration brought squeals of laughter from my friend's mouth and more retching from mine.

As I look back all these years later, a smile forms on my mouth as I fondly remember those few short years my three children were in my care. I'm sure the finger sweep was done many times ... each time revealing a dreaded object to be drug out and tossed in the trash. My mother-arms long to hold the small boy who wept over lost treasure that day and my violating "feener." I shake my head over how quickly those years have come and are now gone.

"What is that in your mouth?" I ask my now forty-one-year-old son, serving his country with six tours of duty in a war zone. He slowly opens his mouth for me to see, revealing sand, sweat, and bitter tears of homesickness as he fights in the war with evil. It is a war that can never be won apart from Christ the peacemaker. I daily beg this Prince of Peace to reign over my son's heart and to cast all fear aside.

"What is that in your mouth?" our heavenly Father asks. He prods our gums and teeth with His holy finger, sweeping to find something dangerous to drag out and toss in the trash. Many are the times He finds ugly words and bitterness hiding behind our lipstick smiles or under a well-groomed mustache ... words as disgusting and unholy as a dog tick in a small boy's mouth.

But today, when our God bends low to search our mouths and sweep with His holy finger, I pray He finds a mouth full of gratitude, prayers, and praise that gush from our lips and spill at His feet, declaring Him holy and worthy—worthy to be praised.

I pray for your sons and mine as a new day approaches, when sand, sweat, and bitter tears are replaced with a new song, even praise to our God.

"Saying, Amen: Blessing, and glory, and wisdom, and thanksgiving, and honour, and power, and might, *be* unto our God for ever and ever. Amen" (Revelation 7:12).

"He brought me up also out of a horrible pit, out of the miry clay, and set my feet upon a rock, and established my goings. And he hath put a new song in my mouth, even praise to our God: many shall see it, and fear, and shall trust in the LORD" (Psalm 40:2–3).

God Remains

Should the sun forbear to shine tomorrow, God will still be God, and I will still be His.

Should trials and temptations come, and should I stumble and fall, God will still be God, and I will still be His.

Should I grow faint of heart and spend a day or long, dark night of the soul in doubt, God will still be God, and I will still be His.

Should there be no morrow, should He come for me in the night, God will still be God, and I will still be His.

"My health may fail, and my spirit may grow weak, but God remains the strength of my heart; he is mine forever" (Psalm 73:26 NLT).

But God remains. What a comforting thought.

The Question of Innocence

"P. J., what was that all about?" I asked my obviously puzzled third-grade son.

He had just taken a late evening phone call from a girl. And after his initial greeting to her, he spoke only one word, over and over again.

"Where?" he asked. A brief pause and then, "Where?"

"Where?" he asked once more. And again, "Where?"

By this time he seemed rather frustrated, and after listening for a minute longer, he very emphatically responded, "Where?" I began to think that maybe something was going on that I should know about. Because of the late hour, I contemplated taking the phone from him. He seemed so frustrated with the young girl who called. But before I could do so, he once again demanded, "Where?"

Finally hanging up the phone, he shook his head and rolled his eyes. "P. J., what was that all about?" I asked my obviously puzzled third-grade son.

"I don't know," he replied. "That was a girl from my class at school. She kept asking me to 'go with her,' but she never would tell me where."

My mouth smiled, my heart sighed, and I silently thanked God for the innocence of my dear eldest son.

"Oh, Lord!" I prayed. "May he always be that innocent!"

"Wherewithal shall a young man cleanse his way? By taking heed thereto according to thy word" (Psalm 119:9).

"Blessed are the pure in heart: for they shall see God" (Matthew 5:8).

Life Is a Gift

Looking out across green fields with sunshine streaming from the sky, I'm reminded what a gift life is. My heart feels light and full to overflowing.

But my days haven't always been that way. Even in the midst of my wonderful, beautiful life, I've felt the heavy sadness of serious depression. My children were very young—three in three years' time. I was one tired momma. Between two surgeries and tons of dirty diapers, with an independent spirit driving me along, I found myself failing at every turn. Postpartum depression wasn't talked about much in those days, but I'm almost certain it had a hand to play in my floundering heart. It was dark behind my eyes even while I stood in the sunlight and cool, happy breezes. I tell you that because I know some of you are there. You are in the deepest, darkest hole the world can imagine.

But look up, my friend, for your redemption draws nigh. The one who created you sees your struggle and longs to help you if you will just look up to Him. Feeling unloved? Ah! Indeed, He hath loved you with an everlasting love. His arms are open for you to run to, to lean on, to hide in. They are your sanctuary—your resting place.

Yes, for certain you may need medical intervention. God has His angels of mercy ready to help you. But don't forget to do your part and look up.

He longs to give you peace and rest, love and light. He will quiet your wresting mind and give you the mind of Christ if you but ask Him.

Yes, ask for wisdom. Ask for His strength, the power of His Holy Spirit. Ask for protection from the evil one—the one who seeks to destroy your soul. Ask for God's perspective … it will change your perception of all that is happening to you. The truth has a way of doing that if we will make it our goal to know Him by personal experience and the reading of His Word. It renews our minds and strengthens our resolve.

Take heart, dear friend. Please do not faint in the way. He came to save you, even from yourself. He came to give you abundant life. Look up, take a deep cleansing breath, sing a song of praise, lift your arms high to the heavens, prepare yourself to receive His blessing, and He will bend down low with His comfort and bless you with joy. I know. I've been there. Look up. The Lord loves you, and I do too.

Life really is such a gift.

> "I will lift up mine eyes unto the hills, from whence cometh my help. My help *cometh* from the LORD, which made heaven and earth. He will not suffer thy foot to be moved: he that keepeth thee will not slumber. Behold, he that keepeth Israel shall neither slumber nor sleep. The LORD *is* thy keeper: the LORD *is* thy shade upon thy right hand. The sun shall not smite thee by day, nor the moon by night. The LORD shall preserve thee from all evil: he shall preserve thy soul. The LORD shall preserve thy going out and thy coming in from this time forth, and even for evermore" (Psalm 121).

I'm Just a Little Girl

It was Saturday, and most Saturdays that meant one thing—chores. Before anything else could happen that day, chores had to be done, or we couldn't make it through the next week without lots of weeping and wailing and gnashing of teeth.

Like most of you with young ones in your home, we were a very busy family. I had a full-time job outside of the home working as an administrative assistant in a government office. My husband was pastoring a church, working odd jobs to make a little extra money, plus he was a full-time student at a university about an hour and a half from our home. We were also the parents of three young children who often went in three different directions. It was chaos. It was hard. It was our life.

This particular Saturday we had more things on our to-do list than could possibly be done, but we had promised the children we would include a few hours of fun if the work was done quickly and without arguments or complaints.

Since the time our children were old enough to toddle and talk, our family scripture has been *"Do all things without fussing and fighting."* It's a loose paraphrase of Philippians 2:14, but one the kids could definitely relate to. They knew all about fussing and fighting, and it was a rarity to make it through a day of chores without someone having a major meltdown. I hated when it was me.

This Saturday was speeding by. The hour was getting late, and the chores were progressing slowly. Very slowly. After what seemed like dozens of trips to my daughter's room to give encouragement, direction, and discipline, my husband was finally at the end of his rope with it all. He firmly told our daughter that she only had fifteen minutes left to get the work done or there would be no fun outing for the evening. She suddenly burst into tears. "But Daddy," she said, "it's too big for me. I'm just a little girl." Stooping down to look in her eyes, he replied, "It's not too big for you because it's not too big for me—I'm going to help you."

Those words rang in my ears last night as I approached the throne of our heavenly Father, crying out about something that is hugely unfair. It's horrible and painful and is way too big for me. This burden carries enormous weight, and it is bearing down on my neck and breaking my heart. "Oh, Father!" I cried out, "please help me. This is just too big for me." As the memory of our sweet girl came vividly to my mind, I continued, "This is too big for me. And I'm just a little girl."

I couldn't see Him do it, but I have no doubt that it happened. The Father stooped down to look into my eyes, and He spoke these words into my heart, "Qené, it's not too big for you because it's not too big for me—I'm going to help you."

We all have problems that seem so big—how can we possibly handle them without His help? He's bigger than any mountain we come up against, and He is strong enough to walk through the valley of the shadow of death with us. When our problems turn into giants, He is bigger still. Thank you, Father.

My husband used to sing this song at church. It was always a favorite of young and old alike!

Bigger Than Any Mountain[8]

By Gordon Jensen

Bigger than all my problems, Bigger than all my fears
God is bigger than any mountain that I can or cannot see
Bigger than all my questions, Bigger than anything
God is bigger than any mountain that I can or cannot see
Bigger than all the shadows that fall across my path
God is bigger than any mountain that I can or cannot see
Bigger than all the confusion, Bigger than anything
God is bigger than any mountain that I can or cannot see

Peace and Quiet

The morning was hectic! Everyone overslept, no one liked their breakfast, voices were raised protesting laundry that had never been washed and drawers and closets that were empty of anything to wear.

One stamped her foot and ran from the room crying loudly! One took advantage of the situation and tried to be boss by slapping, kicking, hitting, and yelling at the other one. (No, it wasn't me. I didn't want to be the boss that day!) And the other one screamed, cried, yelled, and fought off the attacks of the boss.

Somehow, finally, clothed bodies were loaded into the car. It would be only minutes until all were dropped off at school, hopefully to have a good day studying and learning. But during those few minutes in the car, it seemed as if all sanity would be lost as the crying, fighting, and yelling continued. The noise level was unbearable! Unable to concentrate on my driving, I yelled at the top of my voice as I suddenly put on the brakes, stopping dead-still in the road …

"Quiet everyone! You are being so loud that I can't see to drive!"

Suddenly, there was a deafening silence. No one moved. No one said a word. Then, out of the blue, where havoc and rebellion once reigned, there was laughter and giggles coming from the back seat.

"Ha-ha! Momma sees with her ears! Ha, ha, ha!"

Grateful for the change in mood, I continued on to school and gladly watched as my three children ran through the door, laughing and skipping.

I was exhausted! I was a nervous mess! And the noise in my head would not be still, would not be hushed, and would not be quieted.

Have you ever had a day like that? Noise all around? Maybe it wasn't from arguing children. Maybe it was from a television turned up too loud, competing with the stereo or radio. Maybe it was the phone ringing off the hook, and the buzzer on the dryer, washer, and dishwasher all going off at thirty-second intervals. Maybe it was the doorbell ringing, the dog barking, and a neighbor chattering away about trivial nit-picking stuff. Or maybe your spouse was calling down directions to you from upstairs, but with all the noise you couldn't hear or understand.

Sometimes we just need peace and quiet! We need a little stillness to enjoy the sound of the birds singing and the wind whistling. A little quiet place where we can rest and relax to gain our strength back, a haven of silence that we can drink in like a cool cup of water, refreshing our bodies, minds, and spirits.

The scripture tells us that we are to *"be still and know that I am God."* We are to sit and wait on that *"still, small voice"* when God whispers in our ear how much He loves us.

My favorite is this:

"Let not yours be the [merely] external adorning with [elaborate] interweaving *and* knotting of the hair, the wearing of jewelry, or changes of clothes; But let it be the inward adorning *and* beauty of the hidden person of the heart, with the incorruptible *and* unfading charm of a gentle and peaceful spirit, which [is not anxious or wrought up, but] is very precious in the sight of God. (1 Peter 3:3–4 AMPC).

Imagine that! A beauty that doesn't come from face powder and lipstick, braids and hairspray! Just an inner beauty hidden in the heart, charming and peaceful, gentle and quiet! And, did you see it? It said, "Precious in the sight of God!" Precious! Important, valuable, cherished, beloved, dear, and highly esteemed! The Creator of the universe values and cherishes a gentle and quiet spirit—one that isn't anxious and wrought up with foreboding thoughts of pending doom.

I'm holding in my hand a little pair of peace and quiet earplugs. No, they can't shut out all the noise that is in my life, especially the noise that comes from within. But they can remind me to find that quiet place where I can hear from God. And when my heart is uneasy and anxious, loudly crying out for God to help me, they can remind me to be still and trust the one in the universe who isn't ever worried or concerned. You know, the one who is cherishing and highly esteeming the person with the gentle and quiet spirit who trusts in Him.

Shhhh, listen! Do you hear Him? I think He's calling my name and yours!

Read by All Men, Published by None

Some would dare to write a book with many words and wonders printed on its pages. Words that people would devour, consuming them as bread, enjoying them as if drenched with butter and honey. Words, sticky on fingers that must be licked off as a pleasure to satisfy the flesh. Twisting words and turning phrases, all placed just so to tempt the heart, appease the eyes, and speak to the pride of humankind.

Though some might dare, all is folly. True sticky words—words that are sweeter than honey to a person's taste are words that pour as milk and chew as meat. Words that stick to ribs and trim our fat. Words that nourish as wholesome foods. Words that hammer and break the strongest stronghold that isn't God. Words that build and exhort. Words that must drag a person into God's very presence and lay all bare before the throne. Exposing what is for what could be —truth dividing asunder the lie, the life, the what, the if. Sticky words that would cling to gut and break the heart, spilling out the issues of life and changing the hard-hearted person into something they've never seen before—something they've never been.

Ah, but now, he is the book. The Word of life written deep, engrained in flesh and gray matter, making it a home of sorts through which he lives his life. A life read by all people and published by none other than God Himself.

"Pleasant words are as a honeycomb, sweet to the soul, and health to the bones" (Proverbs 16:24).

"Is not my word like as a fire? Saith the LORD; and like a hammer that breaketh the rock in pieces" (Jeremiah 23:29).

"And I will give you a new heart, and I will put a new spirit in you. I will take out your stony, stubborn heart and give you a tender, responsive heart" (Ezekiel 36:26 NLT).

"You show that you are a letter from Christ, the result of our ministry, written not with ink but with the Spirit of the living God, not on tablets of stone but on tablets of human hearts" (2 Corinthians 3:3 NIV).

What Kind of Freak Are You?

I am such a candy freak! I love, love, love any kind of candy, any kind of sugar. I don't buy candy very often in an attempt to take care of the grandchildren's dental health and mine—but when I need a treat, or when I'm in the car on a little journey, candy is in my mouth. It makes me so happy!

As a young girl, I often had candy treats from the little store located in our neighborhood on McCord Street in Neosho, Missouri. My sisters and I loved going to the little store with our pennies clutched tightly in our hands. We would come home with a huge assortment of candy as the little store was a twofer store. You know—a store that sold candy twofer a penny. My favorite was the long black licorice whips that were hard as a stick. To this day I like my licorice stale—it reminds me of the twofer whips I purchased with my precious pennies.

My mom is a candy freak too. We often go to her house on Sunday afternoons between church services. It's not unusual for her to have four or five bags of candy sitting around on the breakfast bar and coffee table. On my way out the door to head back to church, she stuffs candy in my pockets for the hour drive—it's a little journey, and I must have my treats.

My mom's mother, NeeNee, was a candy freak too. I can remember her telling me stories about her growing up years—her family was so poor that they never had any candy. Her treat as a child was a chunk of raw potato. In later years, any time she or my mother was peeling potatoes, all the children would line up to receive their chunk—it became a family tradition. My sisters and I do love our potato chunks, but we love our sweets more!

One summer when I was about ten years old, I spent a week with NeeNee. We would clean her house until it was spotless, and during our work, we would take a fifteen-minute break with a glass of iced Tab or RC cola. During those break times, she would tell me stories about her childhood. I wish I could remember all of those stories, but alas, I remember only a few. I do remember the day she told me, "I don't think I can ever have enough candy. I love it so and never had any as a child." It broke my heart to think that she didn't have candy treats growing up. Even though I ate candy fairly often, I am such a candy freak that I don't think I could ever have enough either.

One of my last memories of my grandmother was when I was twenty-seven years old. I was in the hospital for surgery, and my mother brought NeeNee to see me. It was a difficult trip for her to make—she was very crippled and bent from osteoporosis. As she entered the room to greet me, she handed me a box of candy and insisted that I open it right away. She said it was her very favorite candy that she reserved for special occasions, but she wanted me to have "this lovely box of pastel petit fours" since I was in the hospital. When I opened the box, I could see that it truly was very lovely. What a beautiful box of candy from my beloved NeeNee. During her short visit, all three generations of candy freaks enjoyed lovely pastel petit fours together. We had such fun eating that box of candy! It was the last time I talked and laughed with her. She had a severe stroke and died several weeks later.

So, you see, I truly am a candy freak. Like my grandmother, I love it so! I don't think I could ever have enough candy. Even if I had my share and yours!

Back in the late 1960s and early 1970s, there was a slang term used that I didn't understand at the time—it was Jesus Freak. People who were overly religious and zealous and carried their Bibles everywhere they went were called Jesus Freaks. It seemed so weird to me at the time as that was also a time when drug use and addiction was very common. I always wondered if the two were somehow connected. But shortly after I received Christ as my Savior, I found these verses in the Bible:

• "I beseech you, brethren, (ye know the house of Stephanas, that it is the firstfruits of Achaia, and that they have addicted themselves to the ministry of the saints)" (1 Corinthians 16:15).

• "O how love thy law! It is my meditation all the day" (Psalm 119:97).

• "And they continued steadfastly in the apostles' doctrine and fellowship, and in breaking of bread, and in prayers" (Acts 2:42).

• "And daily in the temple, and in every house, they ceased not to teach and preach Jesus Christ" (Acts 5:42)

• "These were nobler than those in Thessalonica, in that they received the word with all readiness of mind, and searched the Scriptures daily, whether those things were so" (Acts 17:11).

Suddenly it made sense to me. Jesus Freaks weren't addicted to drugs; they were addicted to knowing Jesus and making Him known to others. They were addicted to ministry and prayer and fellowship and God's Word. How wonderful to be addicted to Jesus!

As I think about my health and what my addiction to sugar has cost me, I bow my head in shame. However, my addiction to Jesus will never harm me. His Word tells me that His plan for me is for welfare, not calamity, to give me hope and a future. As I addict myself to knowing Jesus, I am fulfilling the purpose of my life.

Knowing Jesus. There is nothing sweeter than that—not even twofer candy or a lovely box of pastel petite fours!

How about you? What kind of freak are you? What are you addicted to? Are you addicted to Jesus? Do you know Him? And do you want to make Him known to others? I pray you do! May He give us more faith to believe and receive Him into every area of our lives!

Lay It Down!

Even us night owls are grateful when the hour comes that we can no longer stand. It's time to lay it down.

Lay down the worry and the wresting, lay down the fury and the frets, and lay down the broken heart of fear, the shaking confidence, and the wounded pride.

Lay it down. Lay it down. The Savior waits for us to lay it all down. The sorrow of death, the grief of the mourning heart, the broken spirit of despair, the sin-sick flesh that would rather turn its back on God than be slain at the cross weeping for mercy, begging for repentance, pleading for grace. Oh, yes! Lay it down!

It's time to lay it down, for the burdened hands to rest. Let the one who carries our loads fill us with the strength of His Spirit as the heavy eyes close. Let the one who is peace quiet our racing minds, settle the twitching nerves, and still the anxious thoughts. Let's loosen our grips on the day and lay it all down!

Then, as He takes our heavy loads away, may He wipe our bitter tears, frightened tears, lonely tears of pain. Ah, may He soothe our brows with His gentle, holy hand and whisper into the night, "Peace! Be still. Take your rest."

Enjoy your sleep, beloved. May He give us yet another day to love Him and serve Him.

"For I, the LORD thy God will hold thy right hand; saying unto thee, "Fear not, I will help thee" (Isaiah 41:13).

They Played—and We Laughed

I don't know how or when it happened. I only know it did.

The beloved boy with body lank and lean entered this world into my waiting arms and heart hungry for another son to love and hold. The older brother had totally captured our hearts with his beautiful smile and mischievous ways. He was delightful and funny, sweet and precious. We marveled at the blessing of God on our lives. Our joy was so large that only another child could make our lives better. Our first son could hardly wait to have someone to play with and to sometimes tease and torture as older brothers do. Though only slightly older than the wee one, the beloved duo would become best friends. They teetered and tottered through their days, rolling on the floor and holding hands as they taught each other to stand, walk, and run. They played, and we laughed.

In the blink of an eye, no longer than that, it happened one morning while I was folding the freshly washed diapers. I looked up to discover my wee ones playing in the yard and riding bicycles. Sweet-Girl, their beautiful baby sister, was sitting quietly on the steps with her plastic laughing baby. Oh, my, the time had passed so quickly, and our joy was so huge that it was beyond compare! I mused and pondered how quickly all this had happened. With a smile of remembrance and only an ounce or two of regret, I quietly put the diapers away and filled out endless forms enrolling them all in school.

The minutes and hours passed with ball games, Bible school, and swimming lessons. We were stunned at how much we enjoyed this beloved trio, and we laughed at their antics as the days slipped quickly away. With every changing season, they brought us greater joy. Never ceasing to amaze us, they grew in stature and character. We grew children, not grass. They played, and we laughed. We taught them how to love God. We read them Psalms to make them sweet and Proverbs to make them wise. Though we felt as if we had known them forever—only minutes had passed since their births. We were shocked to look up at the end of our busy day and find our first son packing his bags and ready to move away.

High seas and a monster ship had caught this first son's eye. Following in his father's footsteps, he joined the Navy, served our country, and bravely fought for freedom's sake. We were proud, we held our breath, and we missed him. He now has a beloved trio of his own. He raises children, not grass, and he teaches them how to love God.

Not long after, possibly a minute or two, the lank and lean boy with baggy pants and a heart of gold heard the freedom cry of an oppressed nation. He packed away his skateboard, shed his childish ways, and entered the Army to forge a path of his own. He stands straight and tall, strong and brave, as he fights an enemy unlike any other. We are proud, we hold our breath, and we miss him. Soon it will be time to lay his weapon down. He will embrace his wife, play with his children— and laugh.

Sweet-Girl no longer plays with plastic laughing babies. She gave birth to three of her own. She holds them close, afraid to blink her eyes else she should miss this short time with them. She teaches them how to love God. They play, and she laughs. We are proud.

I don't know how or when it happened. I only know it did.

"Train up a child in the way he should go: and when he is old, he will not depart from it" (Proverbs 22:6).

A Tale of the Wedding Dress

I guess I'm a little different than most. As a young girl, I was very shy and terribly backward. I was described as an odd child with strange ways. It seems funny to me now, to type those words, because somehow in the middle of my backward ways, God held me in His hands and carved out a beautiful, wonderful life for me. I live a life of love and joy, strength and courage, qualities that seemed to escape me in my early years of shyness and backward ways. Oh, how good our good God is!

Most young girls dream of their wedding day and plan early on what kind of flowers they will have, who the groom will be, or at least what he will look like. Tall, dark, and handsome is usually the order of the day. But as shy and awkward as I was, I could never imagine having any of those things, certainly not a handsome groom who was madly and devotedly in love with me. Instead of playing dress-up as a lovely bride, I dressed in gowns of sheer curtain panels, fashioning a habit fit for a nun, one who is called to be a different kind of bride—the bride of God, married forever to Christ, and forsaking all other suitors, imagined or real.

No one was more surprised than I was when a handsome young man came fleetingly into my life and stole my young heart of twelve years. And no one was more shocked than I was when that same young man reentered my life at fourteen and was thereafter to be mine forever.

But still, I had no thoughts about weddings or flowers, gowns or bows. My only thoughts were of my bridegroom. He captured my heart entirely, and my eyes were only on him. They still are. They say that on her wedding day "all eyes are on the bride." But that is not exactly true. The eyes of the bride are only on her groom. That certainly was my experience on that wonderful day! My handsome Pat in his Navy uniform totally captured my every look and glance. I barely even noticed the presence of family and friends.

I believe this experience is especially true of Christ's bride, the church. Oh! Don't our eyes glisten and our hearts melt as we anxiously wait for our groom! He is captured in our sight, and we dare not take our eyes off Him as we wait for that glorious day—the day that is yet coming when all is said and done.

Well, this story is not about me. It's not even about my wedding dress. It's about a very special young lady with whom the Lord saw fit to bless my life.

Several years ago, a young man shyly but bravely met with my groom to ask for the hand of our beloved daughter. What strength and courage for one so young to meet with this father, his very own pastor, about such an important request! We marveled at his courage, and we rejoiced that one so young was also very wise. With no hesitation, the blessing was given, and the tale of the wedding dress began.

Our beloved daughter missed those early years of shyness and awkwardness. I love watching her enjoy life with beauty, grace, and confidence. Her inner strength and beauty are captivating, and she is very much her own person, comfortable in her skin.

I was only a little surprised when she told me she was going to purchase a used gown for her wedding. After living in a pastor's home for almost twenty years, she knew that there wasn't much money to spend on those sorts of things. So, she never asked us to buy her a gown. No, she found one on her own that was used and beautiful, fitting her frame perfectly. And she was determined to buy it with her own money.

The gown was lovely. A beautiful ivory satin gown embellished with beads and soutash trim. It looked a little heavy, a little warm for a late June wedding, but it was what beloved daughter wanted, and she was beautiful and happy in it. Only one thing was wrong with the dress. Only one thing marred its beauty. There was a water stain on the train as if the bride who originally wore it was cursed with a rainy-day wedding. But not to worry! Beloved daughter called a local dry-cleaner, and after describing the dress, the beads, soutash, and the stain, she was assured that the dress could be cleaned. "Bring it in the week of the wedding," he said. "We will clean it and hang it for you until the morning of your wedding. Then you can pick it up and not worry about wrinkles or where to hang it. It will be fine!"

With no other thought about the dress, dear daughter went merrily on her way, planning flowers and pew bows, punch and cake, and setting everything perfectly in order for her perfect day.

The Wednesday before her wedding our sweet girl took the dress to be cleaned. Three hours later as I was leaving for the evening church service, she entered the house with tears flowing. She was sobbing and crying as if her heart would break. She took the dress to the cleaners as she was instructed, but upon seeing the dress, the man declared, "I'm sorry, but this dress cannot be cleaned." Twenty agonizing minutes later she left his store to go to another, only to be told once again, "I'm sorry, but this dress cannot be cleaned." Two more stores, two more declarations that the dress cannot be cleaned. She was at wit's end about knowing what to do. She even checked at a local consignment shop to see if they had a dress she could buy. Unfortunately, the only dress they had was not her size and required extensive alterations. What to do? What to do?

With only moments to go before her father, my groom, began to preach the evening church service, we raced to his office for a clear head and advice. Our dear girl entered his office sobbing, "Oh, Daddy, Daddy! I'm so sorry. I did everything I knew to do, but my dress is dirty and stained, and it can't be cleaned." With strong arms around us both, he calmly said, "I'll take care of it." And happily and graciously he sent us to the mall with his blessing and his money to purchase the perfect dress.

We shopped for three hours, and the first dress we saw is the one she bought. It was beautiful, young, and perfect for a late June wedding. No alterations were needed. It was perfect in every way. A clean, beautiful dress provided for a beloved daughter by a father who loves her with an everlasting love.

This little wedding dress tale has come to my mind many times over the years as I consider what Father-God has done for all of us. Weeping over our sinfulness, we entered into His throne room, crying and sobbing, "Oh, Father, Father! I am so sorry. I've done everything I know to do, but my heart is dirty and stained. It cannot be cleaned." With strong arms and a calm voice, the Father replies, "I've taken care of it. I paid the price to make you clean with the blood of my Son, Jesus."

"Thank you, Abba Father! Thank you, Yeshua!"

We live happily ever after. Amen.

"And because ye are sons, God hath sent forth the Spirit of his Son into your hearts, crying, Abba, Father" (Galatians 4:6).

The Beauty of the Lord

I think it's funny when we sometimes say, "I've got to get my beauty sleep." I don't know about you, but most people I know don't look that great first thing in the morning. I know I don't. My hair is usually standing straight on end, and the pattern of my sheets is deeply embedded on my cheeks and forehead. No sir, no beauty in that!

But I do wonder how much of a difference it would make if, at the end of a long, hard day, we would contemplate the beauty of the Lord as we prepare to tuck in and rest in Him. The scripture says, "And let the beauty of the LORD our God be upon us: and establish thou the work of our hands upon us; yea, the work of our hands establish thou it" (Psalm 90:17).

The Lord's beauty is the essence of His perfection. All-loving, all-kind, and full of grace. There is no other equal to our God. And yet, in this scripture, it's a request, a prayer, that the beauty of the Lord would be upon us. It's almost too much to comprehend. For His beauty and His grace to be upon us would mean that we too would be kind, loving, and graceful. We would be covered by Him, dressed as it were, in His holiness.

The second part of this request is that the work of our hands, all we have labored for the day, would be established by the Lord Himself. Without Him, we can do nothing, but He can take the feeble work of our hands and make something successful of it, something that endures the test of time, and something that matters in eternity. He will work it all together, every word, every thought, every effort, and turn it into something that would be for our good and His glory. What a thought!

So, as we stumble off to sleep with the Lord deeply embedded in our hearts, we can confidently pray for His beauty to be upon us, and we can know that He is the only one who can establish the work of our hands.

May it ever be so that we would be like Him. That we would be dressed in His holiness, bearing a resemblance to His beauty, possessing all we need for life and a peace unfettered by the things of this world.

Rest well, beloved. Tomorrow is a new day, and we need our beauty sleep.

An Early Morning Encounter

With a tender heart and tears in his eyes, my husband recounted a father-son encounter he had at five o'clock one morning.

It has been his habit for many years to rise early in the morning. No matter what time he goes to sleep at night, his heart and his mind are wide awake by 4:30 a.m. He is on his feet and dressed by five. He spends those early morning hours with his face in his hands and his heart on its knees, lifting up praise to the Father and requesting mercy and grace, strength and courage, for his family. When I roll over in bed and find him missing, I know that he is sitting in his chair lifting my name up to the throne of grace. Often, I will stir when I feel him rise from the bed, and I mumble a pressing concern. It brings me comfort to know he is praying for our children and me.

One day last week, he rose early as usual for his morning prayers, but while he was praying, he heard a funny little noise. He had left his computer on overnight, and he was getting a signal that someone was trying to reach him on Instant Messenger. When he looked at the screen, he saw that it was our son, Woodi, who at that time was on his third deployment to Iraq.

Anxious to talk with our son, he responded quickly. Suddenly, before his eyes, Woodi's face appeared on the screen! Woodi was trying out a new video program on his computer, and he wanted to make sure it worked before he contacted his wife later in the day. My husband stared into the searching eyes of his second-eldest son, eyes that were searching in the darkness, seeking out his father's face. They had such a great visit with each other. My husband thanked God for the opportunity to remind Woodi of our everlasting love for him and our continued prayers for his safety and quick return home.

Father and son; one on the early side of morning, and the other on the early side of night, each seeking to continue a relationship that cannot be broken by time, distance, or war.

As they bid one another goodbye, and as the father pronounced benediction upon his son, once again my husband bowed his head in prayer and lifted his face to his Father. He now knew what it looked like from God's perspective when his own searching eyes peered out from the darkness into the light of early morning, hoping to find the face of his Abba, Father.

We'll not soon forget this beautiful picture of the Father's love for us, of His desire to see us searching for Him with all our hearts.

When we seek Him with all of our hearts, no matter the time of day or night, we are sure to find Him there waiting for us.

"When thou saidest, Seek ye my face; my heart said to thee, Thy face, Lord, will I seek" (Psalm 27:8).

Here I Am, Lord

Here I am, Lord, the one You love. My face is turned to the skies, and my hands are holy hands as I lift them up high to You, Lord. Fingertips stretching, reaching to the heights of Your heaven, daring even to think that I could touch the hem of Your robe. But, I try, Lord. Every day I try, knowing that my healing is found only in You.

Here I am, Lord, the one You love. You provide all I need for the day and night that stretches forth into a long, hard road. You take my fatigue and overpower it with Your strength. You take my sorrow and infuse it with Your joy. It too becomes my strength, and I no longer plod along, dragging myself to Your throne of grace. No, it is You who lifts and carries me along in a rush of mercy and good will. Ah, I have tasted Your goodness. I have been led with Your kindness. I have drawn close to find You ever near, a present help for my time of trouble.

Here I am, Lord, the one You love. You have filled my life with good things, and there is nothing that I lack. I find nothing of value in this body of flesh, but I find my confidence in You. I find nothing to hope for in this earthy life. Only You, Lord. You are my hope. I hold all things loosely so that I may tightly cling to Your Word. The one You love has placed all faith, all hope, and all confidence in You, the stronghold of my life.

I shall ever be grateful to Yeshua, for it is in Him I live and move and have my being. My beloved Yeshua, the one who loves me and gave His life for me.

"If in this life only we have hope in Christ, we are of all men most miserable" (1 Corinthians 15:19).

A Journey of Purpose

Once upon a time, my family embarked on a new and frightening journey. We left home, church, family, and many people we dearly loved to travel to a faraway place. Our oldest son, P. J., was just beginning his senior year in high school, so it was a tough decision to make. It was only after much prayer and hours of contemplation and interviews that we truly believed God was calling us to make the journey and the commitment to pastor this one particular church. It was a very exciting time for us, even though we were very much outside our comfort zone.

In a year's time there, we had many bad experiences. The worst was when a gang of boys in school severely beat our oldest son. Another was when we took on the local school board for its liberal indoctrination of sixth through eighth graders with a new, ungodly sex education curriculum. But those are another story for another time. Today I want to tell you about one of our first church services that we held for the entire community.

It was a very special service. It was a dedication celebration for a new and very beautiful worship center. And the service was in part special because this church had a new pastor. For over a year, this church was blessed with an interim pastor who was very dynamic and charismatic. What a preacher he was! This church was very proud of their new building and very proud of their interim pastor, so they of course wanted to feature them both on this important day. And they wanted to introduce their new pastor—the new kid on the block. It seemed as if they wanted to find out what kind of stuff their new pastor was made of.

The congregation, being very professional and organized, planned everything down to the second. The service would begin with incredible music by the church choir and praise band. There would be report after report from the various building and planning committees, and there would be a welcome and congratulations from local people who had watched the building and landscaping all come together. The interim pastor would be the keynote speaker, and the new pastor, my husband, would conclude the service. He was asked to speak about the purpose of this body of believers. It all sounded very nice, and my husband was confident he would be able to preach on the given topic until he saw the schedule. After a forty-minute sermon by the interim, my husband would be given five minutes to speak on the purpose of this church.

They waited for his reaction. Would he be upset? Some thought so. Would he refuse to do it? Some thought so. Would he be able to do it? Many doubted it but thought it would be an interesting challenge to watch. In his usual congenial manner, my husband graciously accepted the challenge. "Yes, yes! I can do that. I'll be glad to do that," he said.

Though not particularly nervous that day, my husband was a little apprehensive. It was a tough assignment. We were new in the community. The interim pastor was well loved and such a dynamic speaker. Everyone said so. It was a huge challenge. Could he do it? Or would he fold up? Would they end up firing him just like they did their previous pastor ... the one who was there before the interim? Only time would tell. And it would only take five minutes to do it.

The music was gorgeous, the decorations were impeccable, and the atmosphere was jubilant. The interim pastor? He was absolutely one of the best preachers I have ever heard. He preached flawlessly for forty minutes, and it only seemed like five! He was hilarious, serious, and poignant. He used the scriptures throughout the sermon as if he had written them. His gestures and facial expressions were animated, and they caught everyone up in the joy of the day. He was on top of his game. He was great! Everyone knew it. They waited expectantly for the new pastor to conclude the service.

And what about the new pastor? Would he speak for five minutes and make it seem like forty? Would he be nervous, stumble, and not stay on schedule?

For my husband, it wasn't a contest. He didn't want to be compared. He only knew what God had called him to do, and if he only had five minutes to do it in, so be it. He prayed, "Please, Lord, I only want to honor You. I only want to do a good job for You. I don't want there to be any question in their minds about Your call on my life."

My husband is quite a cutup and has a quick wit about him. After hearing that dynamic sermon and watching it unfold on the stage in such a powerful and dramatic way, his first words were, "I can tell that Brother Fred and I are going to have a strange and wonderful relationship. He is strange, and I'm wonderful." While it was a little smart-alecky of him to say it, it was so unexpected that people laughed and clapped in response. What would this new pastor do for the next four and half minutes? He said, "I've got four and a half minutes to preach a twenty-one point sermon about the commitment of our purpose … Let's go!"

Here is what he said, though he included a few scriptures as he spoke, and he finished exactly on time!

Commitment with Purpose

1. God the Father is the producer, planner, and divine promoter of our purpose.

2. Jesus Christ, the only begotten Son of God, is the person of our purpose.

3. The Holy Spirit is the power of our purpose.

4. Salvation by grace through faith is the possession of our purpose.

5. Eternal life is the promise of our purpose.

6. To be like Christ is the potentiality of our purpose.

7. Living fruitful Christian lives is the proof of our purpose.

8. The gospel of peace is the preparation of our purpose.

9. Being ambassadors for Christ is the profession of our purpose.

10. Being counted worthy to suffer for the sake of Christ is the privilege of our purpose.

11. The good work that Christ has begun in us is the performance of our purpose.

12. Going out into our Jerusalem, our Judea, our Samaria, and unto the uttermost parts of the earth is the plan of our purpose.

13. Building up the kingdom of God here on earth is the progress of our purpose.

14. Winning the lost to Christ is the priority of our purpose.

15. To make disciples of all people is the product of our purpose.

16. Together, every born-again child of God helps to make up the partners of our purpose.

17. The local church is the place of our purpose.

18. Not forsaking the gathering together anytime these doors are open is the program of our purpose.

19. Being able to comprehend with all the saints what is the breadth, length, height, and depth of God's love are the prayers of our purpose.

20. Honoring God in all we do is the praise of our purpose.

21. Receiving a crown of glory is the prize of our purpose.

God will help you do anything if your goal is to bring Him glory. We both made it through that day knowing that God would help us in this place that was so outside our comfort zone. Though I would love to tell you that this was the beginning of a wonderful ministry, I can't.

We were not well received by many in that congregation, but we did what God called us to do and then we came back home.

We are thankful to know that during our time there, many received Christ, and they were all baptized in the name of the Father, and of the Son, and of the Holy Ghost. Amen.

The Cradle Will Rock

As we begin to put this day to bed, it can be hard to shake off the cares of the day. They cling to us like super glue, and the enemy of our souls' delights in our restless sleep.

It is such a great comfort to know that the one who is omnipresent (all present—everywhere at once) is also the one who is omniscient (all knowing). He is also the one who is omnipotent (all powerful). He is described in the Word as the lover of my soul. He delights in blessing His beloved with sleep.

As we close up shop for the day and tuck in tight with Him—that is such a comfort. We can be certain that we are safe in His care. The one who is all present and all powerful—the one who is all—is standing the night watch for us, neither slumbering nor sleeping so that we can. Though it is in my nature to struggle, He has given His life so that I might rest in Him with no worries, no burdens, and no concerns. Just rest. And though the wind may blow and my cradle may rock, I can sleep soundly knowing He cares for me.

He cares for you too. And my prayers for you are going up from the treetop.

"It is vain for you to rise up early, to take rest late, to eat the bread of [anxious] toil—for He gives [blessings] to His beloved in sleep" (Psalm 127:2 AMPC).

I Need Jesus

—✦—

A few years ago, my husband bought a nativity set for me while he was away at a pastor's convention. It's beautifully made of olive tree wood and far too pretty to be stored away in a box. I keep it on a bookshelf in our living room so we can enjoy it year-round.

Tonight our daughter Jené and her family came to dinner for our son-in-law's birthday. It was such a fun and crazy time as my mom and stepdad came too. Our funeral home apartment seems pretty big until you get several adults and lots of little grand-ones running around making noise. It was loud. It was crazy. And the children were very busy!

The youngest grand-one, Natalie, is about eighteen months old, and she is very intrigued with the nativity set on my bookshelf. I think she particularly likes it because she can reach it! Several times tonight we caught her running away from the nativity with baby Jesus clutched tightly in her chubby little hand. Each time her mom would say, "Natalie, go put baby Jesus back in his bed so he can go night-night." And Nat would trot off to put him back in his bed. Minutes later, if she thought no one was watching, she would once again confiscate the sleeping baby Jesus and try to make a fast getaway before being caught.

Finally, Natalie's mom took the baby Jesus from her and said, "No, Natalie. You can't have the baby Jesus to play with." Natalie puckered her lips, and the tears began to flow. Crying, stomping her feet, and reaching high for my daughter's hand in a gimme-gimme sort of way, she sobbed, "Peeees, Mommy, I neeeeeeed Jesus. I neeeeeed Jesus."

The sweetest, truest words ever spoken, "I need Jesus."

How about you? Do you need Jesus?

"Seek, inquire for, and require the Lord while He may be found [claiming Him by necessity and by right]; call upon Him while He is near" (Isaiah 55:6 AMPC).

In Solitude and Silence

A Life Lived in a Funeral Home

In this place where death doth reign, I live amid the reality of vanishing vapors that rise to the heavens to be with God. And I ponder the why, the what, the how—the when.

My own journey has come to a crisis of sorts—a questioning of all I used to know and believe haunts my days and stalks my heart like an unseen enemy.

I long for more of God that I might have understanding and discernment, more of His Spirit that I might not weaken and despair in this interim of circumstances.

I withdraw to hidden rooms to be alone with my thoughts, these sad, solitary ponderings of mine. The solitude lulls my mind to sleep. The quietness drowns my searching thoughts. It is both captivating and chilling to be so alone. I both love it and despise it.

The silence breaks like ocean waves upon a beach—overcoming then retreating, overcoming then retreating. There is some comfort in the repetition of its movements, not unlike the rocking of a mother with her child.

My head on His breast. I rest in His arms. I listen to His heart.

I am certain He has led me to this place, else I could not bear it. I am confident the solitude will bring to pass His purpose for me, revealed in this secret hiding place we share.

This place of death—silent and alone.

This place of life—His heart, my home.

"A time to weep, and a time to laugh; a time to mourn, and a time to dance" (Ecclesiastes 3:4).

I See You—So Does He

Oh, yes! I see you! Did I ever tell you what a wonderful blessing you are in my life? You are a blessing that I never, ever forget to thank God for. Yes, I'm talking about you.

I pray that you will gather all those hard things in your life up into one big bundle and place them at the Lord's feet. You've been fretting and stewing because that is what you do. But God wants you to trust Him. Open your hands. Let go of all the things you can do nothing about. Let go of those things you cling to, and receive the rest that God has for you. Receive His blessing. But you can only receive if your hands are empty.

Why would you hold on so tightly to those hard things when what He wants to give you is so easy, so light? Ask Him to help you see things the way He sees them. Then you will give Him that burden you carry. Then you will release to Him all those things you are so careful about. Ask Him to help you persevere and not faint in the way. He is the way and the truth and the life. No person comes to the Father but by Him, the Lord Jesus Christ. Do not lose hope. He is our hope. The hope of glory. He will only be as strong in you as you are devoted to Him. Why would you choose your strength over His? Yours is nothing. His is everything. It is only when you are weak that He is strong in you.

Ask Him to give you His peace. Did you know that He is our peace? The Prince of Peace. His peace is unfettered by the cares of this world. And when your mind is stayed on Him, He will give you everlasting strength. Strength to let go, not to hang on. All those hard things will still be there, but with His strength, they won't seem so big. He will help you when you release them to Him. He is the strength of your life. Let your only stronghold be Him. Let Him carry that ugly, heavy burden.

Oh, yes. I see you here. And as you've been reading about Him, I've been praying for you.

Have a good rest, beloved. Rest in Him.

"Humble yourselves therefore under the mighty hand of God, that he may exalt you in due time: casting all your care upon him; for He careth for you" (1 Peter 5:6–7).

I'll Never Let Go

We spent the morning walking around the yard picking up things that caught Courtney's fancy and putting them in a basket. A piece of string, an unusual rock, a pop can tab, a red petal from the rose bush, sticks, and stones.

It was such a pretty day. She was so delighted with each item we found that we continued our walk down the lane. It felt sweet, walking along with her hand in mine.

"NéNé, are you holding my hand or am I holding yours?"

"I'm holding your hand, Courtney."

"No, NéNé, I'm holding your hand."

"No, little Courtney, I'm holding your hand."

We bantered this back and forth, continuing our tease until it was time to turn around and walk home.

"I'm still holding your hand, NéNé," she said in a sing-song voice.

"No, I'm still holding your hand, Courtney," I sang back.

"NéNé, don't let go, okay?"

"No, Sweet-Girl. I'll never let go."

Sometimes my relationship with my first grandchild, Courtney, reminds me of my relationship with God. He and I walk together through the day, stopping to examine everything that interests me, treasuring people who have caught my fancy, and enjoying the beautiful scenery along the way. I hold tightly to His hand, and He to mine, vowing that He will never let me go.

Many times over the years I have faltered and fallen, but He still holds me tightly in His hands. I grasp for Him, desperate for His continued presence in my life. His strong arms lift me up, planting me firmly on my feet so that we may continue our walk. My hand in His. His hand in mine.

"Father, don't let go, okay?"

"No, Sweet-Girl. I'll never let go."

"Let love and faithfulness never leave you; bind them around your neck, write them on the tablet of your heart" (Proverbs 3:3 NIV).

"Fear thou not; for I am with thee: be not dismayed; for I am thy God: I will strengthen thee; yea, I will help thee; yea, I will uphold thee with the right hand of my righteousness" (Isaiah 41:10).

That Holy Hand

Ah, that hand, that holy hand that doth bless His beloved with sleep is the same hand, that heavy hand, that doth stop the deeds of evil people.

With one hand doth His strong arm lift up those who have been cast so low, and with the other doth His arm of judgment banish the iniquitor to the depths of the darkest pit.

With one holy hand, He quiets the cries of His children, with the other He turns away those who have not known, have not received, have not believed in the only begotten Son of God. He is not hasty in His judgment, but ever longsuffering that mankind should not perish without Him.

Our God hath revealed Himself to us through the sacrifice of His own Son. His Son, the one in whom there is no shadow of turning, the one who hath been declared the light of the world, that one who hath surely borne our sorrow and sin upon the rugged cross. That one who we love because He first loved us.

Yes, He is that one who is our hope, our peace, the only way to the Father. May that hand, that heavy hand of judgment, also be the hand of mercy. And may that hand, the holy hand, the one that blesses His beloved with sleep, be the hand that wakes us at first morning light to begin the day anew.

May His strong arm lift us up that we might bow low to serve yet another day as He tarries. Oh, dearly beloved! That none should be lost, but that all would be found for our good and the glory of the Father—that is our cry as we rest, as we wake, as we work, as we wait, for one day soon it will be too late. The midnight hour approaches, and this is the day of salvation. Let us rest for a time and then let us be busy about our Father's business.

Grace to you and a peace unfettered.

"O sing unto the LORD a new song; for he hath done marvelous things: his right hand, and his holy arm, hath gotten him the victory" (Psalm 98:1).

It Is Enough

A few years ago, I spent a full day fretting and stewing over a recent turn of events with my husband's job situation. The funding for a ministry Pat was involved in had come to a screeching halt, and in a matter of days one job had ended and he was beginning another—at a much lower salary.

At the time, we were living in a funeral home, and I was managing the office. I had been sick for almost the whole time we lived there. It was an old home, and I felt certain there was something about that building that was making me ill. Fear overtook me many days. I felt if we didn't move soon, I would die in that place. So, we had been looking for someplace to live that was a little closer to Pat's new job. We wanted to buy our own home.

Well, the numbers on the calculator and in the check register just didn't add up. I couldn't possibly see how it was all going to work out. I don't get frantic often. I seldom question God about what He's doing in our lives, but that day just seemed like such a dark, foreboding day in the funeral home. I couldn't seem to lift my head up out of the gloom and doom, and I fretted over what was going to happen to us. Tears puddled in the corners of my eyes most of that day as I pondered our situation and tried to figure out what to do.

Pat was preaching at a little country church that night for a homecoming revival service. It is a church that his grandfather pastored back in 1946–1948. It was an honor to be invited, so even though I wasn't up to it, I attended with Pat. I was very quiet in the car, silently wiping tears away as they poured down my cheeks in the dark.

A woman who lives in the area was leading the worship that night. There was something very stunning about her appearance. She had an energy about her that was captivating! The minute she opened her mouth, we knew she loved the Lord. Her face was shining as she sang that evening.

I was sitting about the third row back, so I could see her very clearly, and I could hardly keep my eyes off her while she worshiped and led us in singing the praise songs. As she played some worship songs on the piano, she would stop singing occasionally to speak as she played. During one such time, she stopped for a minute and read out of Psalm 34:8–10:

> O taste and see that the LORD is good: blessed is the man that trusteth in him.
>
> O fear the LORD, ye his saints: for there is no want to them that fear him.
>
> The young lions do lack, and suffer hunger: but they that seek the LORD shall not want any good thing.

After she quoted these verses, she started playing the piano again. She raised her head and looked directly at me, very deeply into my eyes. It caught me so off guard that it felt like she and I were the only two people in the room.

She very quietly said, "You know that it is a sin to worry. He will take care of you. It doesn't matter what the numbers at the bank say. He said, 'It will be enough.'"

I was stunned! Only God could have told her to say such a thing to me on the very night I had been fretting over His provision for us! Oh! It felt like such a burden had been lifted off my shoulders! And I was so grateful for the Lord's kindness to me. That He would send someone to speak into my life in that way, at that time, was just amazing to me. I knew in that moment how much God cares for me, loves me, and is working all things together for my good and His glory.

The Lord cares about you too. I don't know what you are worried or concerned about, but you do. Perhaps you've been thinking about it all day long, fretting and stewing over what to do, wondering what is going to happen to you. Whatever the problem, whatever the circumstance, let God help you through it. If you are especially concerned about finances, let's take what He said to heart. His provision for you will be enough—because *He* is more than enough.

Let Him be peace in you as you trust Him with your life!

The Kiss

I was tired, discouraged, and depressed. What a busy day at church! We started with sunrise services and breakfast and then finished the morning with Sunday school and worship. We began the afternoon with a service at the local nursing home.

I entered the empty room where we would meet for worship and quietly sat down. Closing my eyes, I hoped a two-minute nap would do the trick and fill me with as much rest as an eight-hour night of sleep. I was weary and fainting in the way. I wished to be anywhere else but where I was.

When I opened my eyes, I slowly looked around the room. I was surprised to see several people waiting for the afternoon worship service to start. My husband was busy digging hymnals out of a cluttered closet, nurses were wheeling patients into the room, and an elderly woman was banging loudly on the piano.

"Anybody here besides me know how to play this piano?" she asked in a loud, scratchy voice.

I rose from my chair and began helping the nurses gather everyone in for worship. Most of the residents were still sleeping with heads bowed and mouths open. Passing by the one or two who were wide awake, I reached for their hands and welcomed them to the nursing home's weekly worship service. I bent down low to look in their eyes and smile, their hunger for love clearly showing in their sad eyes and wrinkled faces.

My eyes scanned the small crowd hoping to see several of our church members in attendance. We had issued the usual passionate plea begging for volunteers to greet the residents with a friendly smile or to sing special music. Ever the optimist, I expected that several would come "to be a blessing and receive a blessing." As I said goodbye at the door of the church that morning, several had promised to come unless, of course, something unforeseen should happen. You know, "the Lord willing and the creek don't rise."

A quick glance around the room left me disappointed and yet thankful. As usual, I was more than disappointed that "the Lord wasn't willing," and yet I was thankful for the two dear ladies who faithfully attended each time our church was scheduled to serve. Judy and Betty were faithful and true, coming to not only greet and worship with the elderly but also to encourage their pastor. They blessed my heart, and I felt more rested by their presence than I did by my two-minute nap.

The service started as we sang a couple of hymns to the tune of the resident pianist banging on the piano and my dear husband following along on his harmonica. Toes tapped, hands clapped, the Word was preached, and the benediction pronounced upon these dear old saints of God.

I felt sorry that most of the residents were still sleeping; many slept through the entire service. Heads bowed, eyes closed, mouths open— it seemed so sad for them to miss this bit of time to interact with other Christians. I silently wondered if anyone had heard the message of hope and encouragement the Lord had for them that day.

Once again, I made my way around the room, pausing for a moment to touch a hand, hug a shoulder, and speak a blessing. I approached the chair of a sleeping resident and briefly considered if I should quietly wheel him back to his room without waking him. But he startled me by reaching out for my hand and pulling me down close where I could see into his eyes.

With tears streaming down his face, he cried, "Thank you so much for coming today. You have no idea how much it means to me. You are a beautiful girl, and I love you for coming to see me."

His shaking hands drew my hand to his lips. He kissed it ever so gently. I instantly knew that the blessing was all mine. Feeling humbled and blessed to be there, I was refreshed by this kind gesture. And I was in tears that his love was greater than mine.

He may have been kissing my hand, but he was really washing my feet.

"For I have derived great joy and comfort and encouragement from your love because the hearts of the saints [who are your fellow Christians] have been cheered and refreshed through you, [my] brother" (Philemon 1:7 AMPC).

Jesus, Mommy, Daddy

I've been reminded several times over the years of something that one of my granddaughters taught me when she was two years old. It's a memory that is very dear to me, and it not only changed my prayer life, but it changed the lives of many people that I do not even know and perhaps will never meet.

This little sweetie-peetie loved to spend the night with us, and there were many Friday nights when sandwiched in between us, she would steal her Papa's space and pillow while kicking me in the face or grabbing all the covers. We loved those sweet times, and they are now among our favorite memories.

One Friday night, we went to bed early. She was cranky. I was tired. We were both a little weepy. In an effort to distract her and calm her down for sleep, I suggested we say our night-night prayers before we tucked in tight with Jesus. With tears flowing down her cheeks, she bowed her sweet little head and simply said, "Jesus. Mommy. Daddy." She soon drifted off to sleep in my arms, and it struck me that such a simple prayer from a child's heart could move the hand that created the universe. She had no idea what to pray for. She just knew that Jesus was the one who would hear and answer.

Many times since that night I've thought about her prayer. What an honor it is to lift the names of our family and friends up to the

Lord. Sometimes I don't know what to ask for, sometimes the need is great, and all that escapes my lips is their names. But I'm reminded that He hears and listens just like He did with a little girl's prayer that night.

I've often thought about the many people in our world who don't have anyone to lift their names up to the Lord in prayer. How do they live without that blessing? What about the person who has never had his or her name mentioned in the same sentence as the name of Jesus? How do the get along? How do they make it through the hard things that happen in their life?

So, I began letter by letter praying my way through the phone book, lifting up names that I do not know to the name of Jesus. "Jesus, Hal Adams. Jesus, George Baker. Jesus, Lyn Carr ..." and on and on it goes. I have no idea how God chooses to bless them, but I do know He does, because it is in His character to love, to save those who are lost, to open the eyes of the blind, to strengthen the legs of the lame, to give hearing to those who are deaf, and to comfort those who are suffering.

I also pray this way for my church family. The eyes of my heart search up and down each pew, calling out their names with the name of Jesus. Then, sometimes people who haven't been to church in weeks will suddenly show up. Sometimes people who are sick will miraculously be well. Sometimes those who are cranky in spirit will sweetly repent and love will flourish. There is such power in the name of our Savior, our Jesus!

Sometimes I pray this way for you. "Jesus, Pris. Jesus, Karol. Jesus, Coco. Jesus, Michelle. Jesus, Shirley. Jesus, Kathi. Jesus, Charlie. Jesus, Kim. Jesus, Trish. Jesus, Willy. Jesus, Sheila. Jesus, Theresa. Jesus, Karissa. Jesus, Mary Jo. Jesus, Dixie. Jesus, Ed. Jesus, Rebecca. Jesus,

Carol. Jesus, Regina. Jesus, Caroline. Jesus, Jeanne. Jesus, Linda. Jesus, Patricia. Jesus, Anjana. Jesus, Cheryl. Jesus, Howard. Jesus, William. Jesus, Kashia. Jesus …" and on and on it goes. Amen.

Where's Your Nose?

It was a clear, cool evening, unusual only in that my husband and I were riding to evening church together. We usually took separate cars as he was often there long before or after I was. But on this clear, cool evening we were enjoying our quiet drive together and the last rays of sunshine that flooded the evening heavens. There's nothing quite like a sunset in the Ozarks. This one was turning white clouds pink against a periwinkle blue sky. It was gorgeous and captivating.

Turning down the country road toward the church, we suddenly came to a screeching halt, turned to look at each other, and then declared in unison, "What was *that?*" Without missing a beat, my husband put the car in reverse, and we sped backward to the strange scene that had momentarily caught our eye.

Staring in disbelief at the unusual sight before us, I once again cried out, "What is *that?*" My husband's reply came through a hint of dismay and a mouthful of laughter.

"Well, it's an animal," he said. "An animal with his head stuck in an ice-cream cup."

By now we were both out of the car and standing at the side of the road, whispering so as not to scare off the strange creature before us. Sure enough, upon close inspection, it obviously was an animal with his head stuck in an ice-cream cup. Melted ice-cream dripped down its body while it stood perfectly still atop an old fence post. What an unusual sight!

"What kind of animal do you suppose it is?" I wondered. Walking around to better size up the predicament, we came to the conclusion that this was a cat. A trapped cat. A cat that was unable to see because of the cup and trapped due to the small hole in the lid where his head was firmly and dangerously lodged.

I don't know why things like that happen when I'm least prepared. I howled with laughter, wishing for a loaded camera to document this strange happening. After a moment or two of examining the situation, I was determined that we had to help this cat! But Pat wasn't so sure.

"It's not going to be easy getting his head out of that lid. He'll rip me to shreds in the process," Pat argued as he considered all his options and his bare arms.

"We can't just leave him there. He'll die. Or something will get him and kill him. How will he eat or drink?" I questioned.

Finally, putting on a jacket he found in the backseat of the car, Pat quietly walked toward the cat. In one swift movement, ready to make a quick getaway, he snatched the cup off the cat's head. The startled cat hesitated for only a moment before jumping off the fence and running through the pasture sporting the clear plastic collar still wrapped around his neck. Ice cream was still streaming down his little ears, and he shook violently trying to rid himself of the cream and the collar. Failing to be fully released, he ran off into the sunset.

We laughed for several moments and wondered what his ultimate fate was to be. I'm sure he had no idea what he was getting himself into when he went into the cup searching for that sweet treat. He had no idea what kind of trouble he could find by putting his nose where it didn't belong.

I wondered about that for several minutes as I waited for my friends' arrival at church for Bible study.

Have I ever ended up in a sticky mess by putting my nose where it didn't belong? Oh, yes. Many times. It's a lesson I've learned over and over.

Have I ever been caught in a trap of sorts, seeking out a sweet treat to satisfy my flesh? One that I knew I shouldn't seek after? Oh, yes. Too many times.

Have I ever been blindsided by something the world offered, taking my attention and eyes off of my life's purpose? Off God's determined plan for me? Oh, yes. It has happened to me.

Have I ever not been able to see my way out of a problem situation, stuck in an awkward position and exposed to whatever evil may befall me? Oh, yes. Time and again, all by my own doing.

Throughout the scripture, the Lord uses many situations and people to teach us these profoundly simple yet seemingly difficult to learn lessons. His warnings are clear. His message is straightforward. His direction is basic and simple:

"Make it your goal to live a quiet life, minding your own business and working with your hands, just as we instructed you before" (1 Thessalonians 4:11 NLT).

- Make it your goal—know your purpose.
- Live a quiet life. When you are quiet, you can hear His voice, and obey.
- Mind your own business. Do not covet what belongs to your neighbor.

- Work with your own hands. Stay busy. If a person does not work neither should he or she eat.
- Read the instructions. Know His Word. Heed His warnings.

I bet if you would ask that cat what he thinks, he would tell you "Don't stick your nose where it doesn't belong."

Nested in My Heart

I love object lessons! Through the years, God has taught me various lessons using simple, common, everyday items that I come into contact with to teach me more about Jesus and my relationship with Him. And over the past thirty-seven years of ministry, he's given me many opportunities to share those lessons with children and adults in various settings. These common, everyday items are no longer common when seen with spiritual eyes and used to convey important biblical truths that help grow me up in Christ and encourage me on my spiritual journey.

For instance, in my Bible I carry a small square of very coarse sandpaper. I use it to remind me that there are people in my life who are sandpaper people. Sandpaper people rub me the wrong way. They often leave scars on my emotions and even on my spirit when I stumble over them, falling in my walk with Christ. Many times though, God uses them to smooth out my rough edges and teach me lessons in humility, mercy, and grace. I keep the sandpaper in my Bible to remind me to pray for these sandpaper people that God allows in my life. I also keep it there to remind me that I am a sandpaper person in someone else's life! It helps remind me to keep my eyes on Jesus, to behave in ways that are pleasing to Him, and to be a blessing to the body of Christ.

Another object I have in my home reminds me of the deep love I am to have for the family of God. It reminds me of people I have come to know who have been an incredible blessing and witness to me ... people who have not just made an impression on my life, but rather people who have had a very profound impact on my life. They are people that God has used to teach me the deep things about Himself that I would have otherwise struggled to learn on my own. This object that reminds me of these wonderful people is a little nester—a nesting doll that my husband purchased on a mission trip to Belarus in 2000.

I love nesting dolls, and I enjoy taking them apart and looking at each doll as it gets smaller and smaller inside the other. One of the dolls my husband purchased had a total of ten dolls all stacked inside of one another. The smallest one was so very tiny that when we dropped it in the carpet, it took five adults several minutes to find it as we pawed and scratched through the carpet fibers! But we found it, and we tucked it safely inside its mother doll, which was tucked safely inside its mother doll.

The reason I love this nesting doll so much is because it reminds me of a beautiful scripture that describes these wonderful people that God has blessed my life with! Here it is in the last part of verse 3 in 2 Corinthians 7 (AMPC): "You are [nested] in our hearts, [and you will remain there] together [with us], whether we die or live."

Isn't that beautiful? Nested in my heart are the wonderful people of God who have walked through my life and made an impact on who I am in Christ, because of their witness and love for our Savior, Jesus!

If you're reading this, then you are one of the people who is nested in my heart. Thank you for blessing my life with yours. Thank you for reading my stories and sharing them.

Pat and I are especially thankful that we recently reconnected on social media with the friends he met in Belarus! They and their families are forever nested in our hearts. We thank God for all He has done in them and through them—what a blessing to call them friends and our brothers and sisters in Christ.

"I thank my God upon every remembrance of you" (Philippians 1:3).

In the Night Watch He Loves Us

Beloved, may the Lord be ever gentle with us and gracious about our faults as we lay it all down. As we tuck in tight with Him, may His rest become ours and the strength of His holy arm hold us up in our weakness.

May He ever instruct us in the night watch as we open our hearts to Him. As we quiet ourselves in His love, may we hear His voice clearly speaking peace, light, and love over our fretting hearts. At the end of this day, may we know that He kept us from every evil. No matter our circumstances or burdens, may we know that He has truly been good to us. Even in those hard places, He has walked with us and carried us when need be.

What is it that you need to lay down to find His peace? Lay it down, and let it go! Find a peace unfettered by your worries and cares as you rest in the everlasting arms of our Savior.

We are blessed. We are blessed with His rest, friends. The Lord loves you, and I do too.

"For thus saith the Lord GOD, the Holy One of Israel; In returning and rest shall ye be saved; in quietness and in confidence shall be your strength …" (Isaiah 30:15)

Go Ahead—Pour Yourself Out! He'll Pour Himself In!

Have you ever poured yourself into doing something for your family, your church, or God only to be misunderstood by others? Have you ever felt the sting of their indignation or heard the murmured complaints of others as you gave your all for them? Have you seen the raised brow, the critical eye, and heard the click-click-click of tongues from little groups who gather in dark corners? Perhaps you have even been questioned about your intentions and wrongly judged for your motives?

If so, you are in good company. There was a woman such as that in the ancient town of Bethany. She dared to give the Lord all she had and more. Offering up a sweet-smelling sacrifice, she lavishly poured expensive perfume over the Lord's head. The community of faith didn't understand. They didn't see the worthiness of the Lord or the depth of her love. They only saw her extravagance and assumed it was waste. They rose in bold opposition to her and berated her actions in front of the one who was soon to die for their sin, and ours.

But Jesus bid them to let her alone and trouble her no more. In fact, He raised a memorial to her for all generations, and we read it in His Word yet today. How she must have wept at His feet to hear Him proclaim her blessing. How she must have loved Him all the more to hear Him declare in her defense, "She hath done what she could."

Perhaps you hear the murmurings of opposition in your ears today— the naysayers questioning your love, attacking your faith. The opposing words may even come from your own legalistic heart, as you fear you must do more and more to earn His love. But His love cannot be bought —it is freely given to all. And to those of us who are willing receive it, we simply present our lives as a living sacrifice, pouring ourselves out as He pours Himself in. It is our reasonable service. It is His mercy and grace.

At the close of the day, with our heads on the pillow, the Holy One stands in our defense protecting us from the voice of condemnation. He lifts us up with His strong arms. As we drift off to sleep in sweet peace, we hear His voice speak into the night, declaring, "Let her alone and trouble her no more."

"Yea, she hath done what she could."

> "After two days was *the feast of* the Passover, and of unleavened bread: and the chief priests and the scribes sought how they might take him by craft, and put *him* to death. But they said, not on the feast *day*, lest there be an uproar of the people.
>
> And being in Bethany in the house of Simon the leper, as he sat at meat, there came a woman having an alabaster box of ointment of spikenard very precious; and she brake the box, and poured *it* on his head. And there were some that had indignation within themselves, and said, why was this waste of the ointment made? For it might have been sold for more than three hundred pence, and have been given to the poor. And they murmured against her. And Jesus said,

Let her alone; why trouble ye her? She hath wrought a good work on me. For ye have the poor with you always, and whensoever ye will ye may do them good: but me ye have not always. She hath done what she could: she is come aforehand to anoint my body to the burying. Verily I say unto you, wheresoever this gospel shall be preached throughout the whole world, *this* also that she hath done shall be spoken of for a memorial of her." (Mark 14:1–9)

"I beseech you therefore, brethren, by the mercies of God, that ye present your bodies a living sacrifice, holy, acceptable unto God, *which is* your reasonable service" (Romans 12:1).

Let It Go! Let It Go! Let It Go!

Sing to the tune of "Let It Snow! Let It Snow! Let It Snow!" You get the drift.

A funny thing happened in my pew one Sunday. My daughter and her family were visiting for the weekend, and one of the highlights of their trip was when they attended church with us. So, with five-year-old Allison and two-year-old Isaac in my pew, it was a pretty happening place!

I gave Allison Qené a dollar bill to put in the offering, and I also gave her one for Isaac, who was sitting on my daughter's lap. Like all children, she was very excited to have real money to give to God, and she hurriedly explained to Isy what he was to do during the offertory.

"It works like this, Isy. You see those big golden plates on the table? When they pass you those plates, you put your money in. This is the way you gotta do it. You just gotta put it in, and let it go!"

Funny how a five-year-old can grasp a spiritual truth better than most adults! "Put it in, and let it go." No strings attached. No longing gaze as you watch your money go on down the aisle from person to person. No reaching in and taking it back. No making change out of the offering plate, trying not to give more than you have to … more than is required. Just putting it in, and letting it go back into the hands of the one who gave it to you in the first place.

I thank God for the trusting innocence of children. I pray my own heart always has such pure love, joy, and motive! I pray yours does too. May we be blessed with a faithful heart and a generous, open hand.

"Let each one [give] as he has made up his own mind and purposed in his heart, not reluctantly or sorrowfully or under compulsion, for God loves (He takes pleasure in, prizes above other things, and is unwilling to abandon or to do without) a cheerful (joyous, "prompt to do it") giver [whose heart is in his giving]" (2 Corinthians 9:7 AMPC).

The Last Thing
Life in a Funeral Home

Alone in the darkness, in the silence of this place I call home, I sit for many minutes struggling with my thoughts. It seems so incredulous to me, so bizarre. And yet, I know it to be the truth of the way things are ... and I must tell you.

But how do I tell you this? How do I put into words what my eyes have seen? How do I give utterance to that which is unspeakable? To that which some might find horrific? But to that which no other beauty can be compared?

I must tell you. And you must know, else you should die and never know how it will be for all of us.

The story really begins in 1905. A sweet baby girl was born to live ... until she died. The fact that 102 years passed from the beginning to the end seems most remarkable.

Such a pretty woman; her skin, smooth and taut, belied her age and left no telltale signs of a first husband lost at sea. She was left alone to raise two small boys, barely more than a child herself. In time, another husband brought joy and laughter to the once grieved widow ... and more children. The years spent in happiness slipped by one by one. She built a life and grew a legacy; she was strong, she worked hard, and she knew God. She raised children and a garden. Somehow she outlived them all, friends and family alike.

Though strong in spirit, she was frail in body. Thin as a wisp, she was a tiny woman with a crooked back and crippled feet. It was early last Sunday morning when she had finally done all she could do. The Lord called her home, and she gladly went without packing her bags or looking back. She left it all to follow Him home.

Today was an important day for her—her final bath, her final dressing, the final brushing of her soft gray hair. The young man of near thirty years took such care to make things right, to make them just so. And when she was ready, when all was in place, he lovingly picked her up in his arms as a groom carries his bride. He carried her over the threshold to the place where her casket-bed was waiting. Very gently and tenderly he tucked her in, smoothing her garments and folding her hands. As he patted the last curl loosely in place, he turned from his work and was startled by my presence in the doorway.

Seeing my wondering eyes, he simply said, "It's the last thing that human hands will ever do for her."

It seemed as if he had been born for no other reason than to do this one last, kind deed for this dear old saint of God.

It left me stunned, knowing that in hours or days, months or years, this is the way it will be for me. This is the way it will be for you.

"Precious in the sight of the Lord is the death of His saints" (Psalm 116:15).

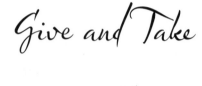

Give and Take

The sun has set. The shutters are closed. The door is locked up tight with my prayers—and I'm tucking in tight with You, Lord.

Please. Take my worry and care and cast it to the bottom of the sea, never again to be fretted over and wrestled with by me.

Please. Give me a clear mind, a pure heart, and a desire that longs to please only You, God—hearing only Your voice as You call me out of the crowd.

Please. Take the busyness that wrangles my peace with twisting fingers and a shaken faith that makes no time for You, Lord. The noise of my rebellious spirit rings in my ears and troubles my heart. Replace it, Lord, with a quiet obedience that can only be found as I rest in You.

Please. Give me understanding and knowledge about Your will for my life. Let me see from Your perspective, Lord, not my own, which is skewed from living in this world of sin. Help me discern spiritual things—things about You. I want to know Your secrets, the better part … things that can only be learned by spending time at Your feet.

Please. Take my weakness and replace it with Your power. Be strong in me. Bless me with perseverance and patience as You work Your will and way into my heart for my good and Your glory. Take me out of the darkness that I might walk with You in the light. Lift me up with your strong arm and make my footing sure as I walk in the narrow way. The way that leads to You, Lord—the one who is the way. Take it all, Lord, and give me You.

Please. May it ever be so.

"...the Lord gave, and the Lord hath taken away; blessed be the name of the LORD" (Job 1:21).

Home

There is a lovely little city in the southwest corner of Missouri. On the map, it's known as Neosho, but I call it *home*. As we enter the city limits, I feel like I am being hugged by memories, both good and bad. The city wraps its arms around me and whispers in my ear, "Home. This is home." Just thinking about it brings such emotion to me that I cannot keep the tears from puddling in my eyes or a lump from forming in my throat. As we drive through the streets, my eyes search unceasingly for those sites that are so loved and familiar to my heart.

For several months, we planned to make a move to Neosho, Missouri, where my husband and I grew up together. I was very excited because my mother had just recently moved back to the area after spending most of thirty years in Arizona. Neosho would locate me equal distances between my mother and my children and grandchildren. Either relationship would only be an hour away—perfect! A few things had to fall into place financially, but it seemed as if it would all work out.

My husband and I drove the streets many times throughout those months searching for a house to call our own. I could imagine myself in each one of the houses we looked at—working in the kitchen, playing with grandchildren in the yard, and making up the beds with sunlight streaming through the window. I imagined long walks with my husband into the center of town where we would stop at stores around the square to greet people we knew from long ago. It seemed so perfect. But God has other plans for me, and my dream is not to be, at least for now.

"For I know the thoughts and plans that I have for you, says the Lord, thoughts, and plans for welfare and peace and not for evil, to give you hope in your final outcome" (Jeremiah 29:11 AMPC).

As we were making our plans to move to Neosho, we enjoyed several days and evenings as we drove around town and walked through the square remembering old times. This is the city my husband and I grew up in, the place where we met and fell in love at the tender ages of twelve and fifteen. This is the place where one of our babies was born and where we raised our three children in the early years of their lives. It is *home*.

I did a little research, noting the growth of the city, and poured over maps and history books tracking an area in which we would like to live. A street behind the church I grew up in has several houses that have always intrigued me, and from time to time I would know some of the people who lived in those houses.

Years ago I heard an interesting story about the name of that street. It seems there was a certain well-known woman who lived on that street. Her family had lived in the city from its beginning years. On a shopping trip to one of the larger cities in the area, she was writing her name and address down for one of the department store managers. He glanced at the address as she handed it to him, and he said, "It must be nice to live on Easy Street." Several people nearby heard his remark and laughed, but the woman was offended. Yes, she did live on Easy Street, but there was nothing easy about it. She and her family had worked very hard throughout the years to help make Neosho a nice place to live and raise families. But Easy Street made it seem like they were lazy and knew nothing at all about hard work.

Without wasting any time when she returned home, she went to the next city council meeting and requested that the street's name be changed. And it was. The street has been known as Rockhill Road since that time.

I love that story, not just because it's an interesting piece in the puzzle of Neosho's history, but because it contains so much truth that can be applied to each of our lives.

Many people who have received Christ as their Savior believe that their lives will now be easy, and they will no longer encounter trouble as the world does. Even those of us who know there will still be trouble are sometimes in disbelief at how much trouble can enter our lives. And seemingly it lasts for a season with many trials and temptations coming our way all at the same time. Sometimes our prayers go unanswered, and we begin to doubt. Sometimes we struggle between the weights of enough and lack, and we allow our faith to be crushed and tested to the limit. Sometimes our prayers are answered, and God says no. We might even believe that He doesn't understand our situations or care about our problems, and we struggle in the way.

The truth is, there is no Easy Street. But there is a Rockhill Road, which at times is difficult to climb. It seems there are many rocks on the way— each one an obstacle to our faith, each one potentially causing us to trip and fall. During these times, we must draw near to Him because He does not have evil planned for our futures. But He does have a plan of peace for us, a plan of good welfare that will be for our benefit and His glory.

I'm not sure where the Lord is leading us, but I know it will not be to Neosho. He has stopped us at every turn and will not provide a way for us to live there. The scripture assures me that His thoughts toward me are good and not evil. They are thoughts of peace and will bring me to an expected end—an end that He has planned just for me. So, I trust Him. And I wait—knowing that my real *home* is heaven.

If He Did Not

Our Yeshua is such a precious friend to us. The strength and depth, the height and width of His love overwhelms us. We are left in tears that such a beautiful holy love would endure such a horrible death for us. But we would be in such despair if He did not. Oh, who would care for our souls if He did not? Who would dare to die for our sin if He did not? Who would lavish us with pardon and favor, His unmerited grace, if He did not?

Oh, beloved, we would be in such a sorry state if He did not. But He did. God saw fit to give us Yeshua, our beautiful Lord, the lover of our souls. Thank you, Father. Just give us Jesus for all of our sorrows and despair. He is our precious friend, our Savior, and our king.

Don't let the problems and mournings of life discourage and defeat you today, beloved. Just think of Him and be overwhelmed with His love, His peace, His power. Let Him speak life into your circumstance, and He will make a way for you where there seems to be no way.

Thank You, Lord! You are such a gift to us. As we tuck in tight with You, give us more faith, more love, more strength, more joy, more peace. Oh, yes! Give us a peace unfettered by this world of fears. Prince of Peace, please draw near.

"Thanks be unto God for His unspeakable gift" (2 Corinthians 9:15).

Ah, Such Relief!

Sometimes late at night when the day would seem most spent, emptied of all it can hold, that's when the Spirit of the living God begins to move upon our hearts. His stirring starts gently, wooing us to be quiet before Him. His soft, compelling voice begins to call, and we stop to listen closely for our names.

We think we can hear Him speak as the noise of the day leaves us. And suddenly we find ourselves encompassed by His love. It hovers over us, covering from our sight all those things that seek to crowd Him out. His strong love compels us to draw nearer still, and it fills us up to the brim with His goodness and mercy.

The hardships of the day begin to leave us, dropping as heavy baggage that we can no longer carry. The peace we feel is so sweet that we gladly fling away all that ties us to the perils of this world. Ah, such relief! We find the peace we've been longing for, so we lean in tight as He lifts us up with His strong arms. And our eyes grow heavy with His rest. We trust Him with all our cares.

Beloved, what is it tonight that is keeping you from hearing His voice? What burden can't you lay down or fling away so that you can draw close to Him? Let Him lift you *up*. He will never let you down. Tuck in tight with Him and enjoy your sweet rest.

"I lie awake thinking of you, meditating on you through the night. Because you are my helper, I sing for joy in the shadow of your wings. I cling to you; your strong right-hand holds me securely" (Psalm 63:6–8 NLT).

The Intruder

Silently, slowly he entered my room, 'bout half-past midnight last eve, bringing with him a cloak of cold air to place heavily over my sleeping frame.

So skilled in his step was he that I took no notice when he made his way across the wooden floor and then hovered and perched on the side of my bed. With long, cold fingers, he touched my brow, gently stroking my face, my neck, my breast. It was only then that I opened my eyes, wildly startled by his presence.

Struggling to see in the dark, I felt him rather than saw him—his presence like a heavy weight bowing low upon me, his large form dark and foreboding.

I was so overcome; I dared not, could not speak.

My body trembled uncontrollably beneath this middle-of-the-night intruder. It seemingly brought him great pleasure to feel my terror, and he drew closer still, continuing his caress.

Sweat poured from my brow. Tears flowed from my eyes as I struggled beneath the force of his weight. My breath was but a gasp from my lips, loudly filling the dark room with its sound.

Finding voice and courage in a moment of desperation, I spat out, "Your name. Your name! I must know your name and what you want of me." I thought I should die if I did not know—surely, I would if I did not speak. We struggled again. The strength and determination with which he attacked my body were more than I could fight against.

Again, "Your name. Please! Tell me your name and why you have come." I wept and choked as I spoke, certain that I was about to die at his hand.

He leaned into me, close and smothering, his voice rasped harshly against my ear. He had the smell of death about him, and his long, cold fingers clutched at my breast as if to tear my heart in two.

Alas, a sharp revelation! Oh, my! Could this possibly be? How could it be that as he spoke, I realized I knew him well?

He had been here in my home many times! In fact, I had entertained him lavishly throughout that very day. I shrank from his deadly grasp as his spoken name entered my ear and ripped at my heart.

"Fear!" he declared. "My name is Fear. I have come to steal, kill, and destroy your rest, your peace, your hope. Where is He, this one whom you claim to know? Where is He in your hour of deepest need? Could it be He knows of your wretched, wicked heart? You are worthless. You are shameful. You are undeserving of His love and care. Hath He not forgotten you? Hath He not forsaken you? Have you not been rejected by both man and God? Will you not be poor and homeless and pitifully sick all the rest of your days?"

His words tore deep into my heart; his hatred for my life smothered the weakened breath lingering on my lips. I was powerless against his advance—but the Spirit of the one who died for me arose up in the dark of night! Somehow my tongue gave utterance to His name.

"Jesus." As I spoke His name, this midnight terrorist released his grip on my heart.

"Jesus." As I spoke His name, this intruder from hell shrank from my sight, disappearing into the night.

"Jesus." As I spoke His name, the Prince of Peace healed my wounds and washed my feet.

The words came slowly at first and then scrolled faster and faster through my mind as if it were the writing of a scrolling marquee ...

I will never leave you, nor forsake you ... Everyone who calls upon the name of the Lord shall be saved ... Greater is He that is in you than he that is in the world ... At the name of Jesus, every knee shall bow of things in heaven, and things in earth, and things under the earth ... He will keep you in perfect peace whose mind is stayed on Him ... For there is one God, and one mediator between God and men, the man Christ Jesus ... I have come that ye might have life, abundant life ... I have never seen the righteous forsaken nor their children begging bread ... I am the way, the truth, the life, no man comes to the Father but by Me ... I will bless your bread and water and take sickness far away from you ... For thus saith the Lord GOD, the Holy One of Israel; in returning and rest shall ye be saved; in quietness and confidence shall be your strength ... I know the plans I have for you, plans for health and welfare, plans to give you a hope and a future ... No weapon that is formed against thee shall prosper, and every tongue that shall rise against thee in judgment thou shalt condemn ... This is the heritage of the servants of the LORD, and their righteousness is of me, saith the LORD ... Perfect love casts out fear ...

Jesus. Jesus. Jesus. Both the night and my heart returned to quiet rest. Dear Jesus had once again rescued me from a deadly attack of *fear*.

"For God hath not given us the spirit of fear; but of power, and of love, and of a sound mind" (2 Timothy 1:7).

"The name of the LORD is a strong fortress; the godly run to him and are safe" (Proverbs 18:10 NLT).

A People with Hope

Lord, if You hadn't helped us, there's not even one that would have made it through the day. If You hadn't provided a shield of protection, we can only guess at the evil that would have befallen us. If the strength of Your Spirit had been removed from this world, the ensuing chaos would have been more than any person could bear. If You hadn't filled our lungs with air, our bodies with life, and our spirits with Your Holy Spirit, we would have been as a vapor that vanishes with the winter wind, void of all hope of eternal life.

There is no relief for that kind of misery. But, in Your infinite grace and mercy, You kept us from that sorrow and gave us glad, joyful hearts, saving us even from ourselves.

Father, if You hadn't sent Your Son, Jesus, to die for us and raised Him up from the dead by Your power, we would be a people most miserable—people without hope, without peace, without joy, and without salvation.

Thank You for Your help today, Lord. Thank You for Your pardon, protection, provision, power, and peace for life. We ask that You bless us with Your perspective and perseverance that we may please You in all things until that day You call us to be at home with You. Help us to rise above the circumstances of life and see things the way You see them—give us the mind of Christ. And we pray that tonight as we rest, You will draw near, and we will rest in You.

Blessings of love and prayers for you, beloved.

"Arise, shine; for thy light is come, and the glory of the LORD is risen upon thee. For, behold, the darkness shall cover the earth, and gross darkness the people: but the LORD shall arise upon thee, and his glory shall be seen upon thee" (Isaiah 60:1–2).

"For you bless the godly, O LORD; you surround them with your shield of love" (Psalm 5:12 NLT).

A Day with Friends

———✦———

I love Saturdays! I spent time with some friends today. It's always good to see them, and it took only a few minutes of easy banter before we all settled in, comfortable with one another's presence. Before long, it was as if we'd never been apart. It was as if we'd seen one another only yesterday. You know how it is with friends. We each have our stories to tell, talking over one another, teasing and laughing at crazy, outrageous things that happen in everyday life.

The easy conversation and laughter relaxed me so that I momentarily closed my eyes to take it all in. As I listened to them talking, my breathing was slow, measured, and deep. I buried myself in their words, and suddenly it was as if I was flying in the sunshine, out of my body, out of time … alone with them in another world. No one else mattered, and the wind became my wings. The sunlight was my strength. They lifted me up and took me far, far away to another place, another time when our lives were simple, slow, exciting, and beautiful. They took me back to yesterday. My friends' memories became mine.

As they shared their stories, I felt like I made new friends with everyone they know, everyone they talked about. Oh, I knew them only for this moment, but it seems that I will love them forever. When they laughed, I laughed. When they wept, I wept. And when their lives crashed, and they could bear no more, I bore it for them and begged them to be strong, to live in peace, not to let go, to carry on no matter what.

In just that short time, that short visit, we traveled to exciting places together … places I've never been. But they showed me the way, drew me into their circle, and introduced me to their friends. Their family became my family, and I joined in. We sat at the table as we ate and drank, discussing world affairs, politics, and religion, husbands and babies, careers and dreams. They were loud and boisterous, sarcastic and funny. And I sat silently by, smiling, watching, listening, growing, learning … enjoying their lives, and their stories. I am so thankful to know them. What kind generosity to share their lives with me.

All too soon it was over. It was time for my friends to go.

Then I turned the page, and I closed the cover. I just read a book.

But Not!

The Christian life is such a paradox. It sometimes seems particularly so for those of us who have devoted our lives to ministering in and to the church. Paul describes it very well:

> We are hedged in (pressed) on every side [troubled and oppressed in every way], but not cramped *or* crushed; we suffer embarrassments *and* are perplexed *and* unable to find a way out, but not driven to despair; We are pursued (persecuted and hard driven), but not deserted [to stand alone]; we are struck down to the ground, but never struck out *and* destroyed; Always carrying about in the body the liability *and* exposure to the same putting to death that *the Lord* Jesus suffered, so that the [resurrection] life of Jesus also may be shown forth by *and* in our bodies. (2 Corinthians 4:8–10 AMPC)

It's funny how two small words can give us such hope.

- But not crushed;
- But not in despair;
- But not deserted;
- But not destroyed.

If not for the "but not," I would be such a mess! I thank God for the encouragement we find in His Word and at His feet!

I am tired … but not exhausted (completely used up!) May we all rest well in Him.

"He will not suffer thy foot to be moved: he that keepeth thee will not slumber" (Psalm 121:3).

A Midlife Crisis

Ugh! Lately, I just can't seem to get a clear thought in my thick skull. My thoughts are as big of a jumble as the top drawer of my desk. And I have dozens of conversations and to-do lists darting around in my head like bullets.

Does that ever happen to you?

That happens to me a lot since I passed the "5-OH!" marker a few years back. It is part of that middle-age thing everyone talks about. Body parts seem to get slower and lower, and nothing works the way it used to or is supposed to. Whoever said that midlife crisis is about short skirts, hot mamas, and younger men with fast red cars is just wrong! No! It has nothing to do with all that.

Midlife crisis is about slow, stiff joints; it's about not being able to hold your water, losing track of what day of the week it is, and finding your purse in the refrigerator.

It's about not being able to remember the grandkids' names and calling one of them Alex when the truth is you don't know anybody named Alex.

It's about line jumping at Wally-World and having to leave your cart mid-aisle to avoid embarrassing yourself with wet pants or loose bowels. Or both. It's about thinking you're in Mexico when really you're in China.

Midlife crisis is about long, prayerful nights when you find out your fifty-eight-year-old spouse is suddenly unemployed. It's about learning to trust God when the bank says you are out of money, but the gas pump says $4.00 per gallon. It's about watching the slow and halted step of your spouse, wondering if he's sick or tired—but knowing in your heart that he's both. It's about needing to sit down for a year or two to catch your breath and the realization that you can't sit down because you're only halfway through.

Midlife crisis is about pulling yourself up by the bootstraps, and whether you feel like it or not, doing it all anyway. It's about playing on the floor with the grandchildren and collapsing when their parents take them home. It's about holding onto each other's hand so that neither of you will fall. And if you do fall, it's about knowing that you won't go down alone.

It's about faith, enduring faith that never, ever gives up on life—this one or the next. It believes that God still has a plan for you, and work for you, and a mission for you.

Midlife crisis is the blessed assurance of knowing that it's not over until *He* says it's over. It's about knowing that God has your days numbered, and you won't live one day longer or less than the days He has marked out for you.

A midlife crisis isn't a crisis at all, because you trust God—even when you find your purse in the refrigerator.

"So teach us to number our days, that we may apply our hearts unto wisdom" (Psalm 90:12).

He Maketh Me Dance!

Sometimes without any warning, a gut-wrenching sob finds its way out of my heart and into my throat. I know not from whence it comes, other than that deep place within where only God can see. It always takes me by surprise—the strength of that emotion—and before I realize it, it has escaped my lips and floats through the air like a deep, anguishing cry, like that of a wounded animal.

A cry for what? Again, I know not. An emptiness perhaps, a homesickness for heaven, I sometimes suppose—a longing for something more of Him. Only He knows.

He reads my thoughts like a book, and He knows my heart as the lover of my soul. I only know that I must bow low to ground to touch His robe and strike my breast for mercy.

I close my eyes and imagine myself at His feet, reaching with one hand to touch His hem and with the other I beg for His attention. The God of all comfort speaks to me at these times with grace and mercy flowing from His throne, comfort and love flowing from His heart. With His strong arm, He picks me up and lifts high my hands, which hang down, and He strengthens my feeble knees. With His mighty power, He fills me with confidence. Within the shadow of His wings, He hides me from the evil one.

A mighty fortress is my God where I find all that I need of Him. The air is no longer filled with the sound of my weeping, but rather a shout of joy rings through the night and praises of joy flow from my lips like that of a laughing, dancing child.

"Hear, O LORD, and have mercy upon me: LORD, be thou, my helper. Thou hast turned for me my mourning into dancing: thou hast put off my sackcloth, and girded me with gladness; To the end that my glory may sing praise to thee, and not be silent. O LORD my God, I will give thanks unto thee forever" (Psalm 30:10–12).

Stranger Danger

I was reminded of a really silly bathroom story today, and I think it will make you laugh. You could use a little laugh, yes?

Several years ago, we were on a road trip with our daughter and church family. We had spent the week in Wyoming helping a little church with their vacation Bible school and a community block party in the park. It was fun. It was hard work. We were very tired.

On our way home, we decided to drive through Colorado to enjoy the scenery and visit some friends. It added a few hours to our trip, but it was worth it. The extra hours in the car pushed me from tired to exhausted. I'm not a good traveler.

One evening we pulled off the highway in a very small town to use the bathroom and refuel—with candy, not gasoline, because I've got to have travel treats! It was such a small convenience store that I was sure there was only one stall in the bathroom, so my daughter decided to stay in the car sleeping a bit while I went in to use the ladies room. We had played out this tandem potty-party many times over the previous week, and I cautioned Noni to keep the car doors locked until I returned.

I was surprised when I entered the bathroom that there were actually two stalls. It seemed that someone was in one of them, so I hurriedly went in the other. I had been holding it for many miles and was desperate to get my business done. As I sat there, I had such a strange feeling like someone was watching me. I was very uncomfortable and looked up toward the ceiling, examining the room a bit. When I did, I was surprised by a funny little window on the left side of the stall! It was about twelve by twelve inches squared. And the woman in the stall next to me was watching me!

Startled, I let out a little scream and looked away, grabbing toilet paper to finish up my business and get out of there. Through the corner of my eye, I could still see the woman watching me through the corner of her eye. I was freaked out. I decided to say something.

"Oh! You scared me. I wasn't expecting a window in the bathroom stall. Isn't it the strangest thing you've ever seen?" I said with a shaky voice.

She said nothing. I noticed she was still watching me. Trying to clean up and be modest was a little hard to do in such a small space, and she was obviously determined to violate my privacy.

"I'll hurry up and let you have the bathroom all to yourself," I stated. "It's a little disconcerting knowing someone can see you, isn't it?" I privately hoped my pleasant chatter would keep her from murdering me in my stall.

She said nothing. I flushed and quickly exited the stall stopping only to briefly wash my hands.

"Have a nice evening," I said. "I'll pray for your safe travels." Pulling open the heavy, dirty door with a paper towel in my hand so as to not to touch anything, I ran out of the room.

When I reached the car, I nervously told my daughter about the strange encounter in the bathroom and asked her to wait a few minutes before going in. But she had to go now! And she assured me she would be okay since I made it out alive.

"What did you think about that strange woman?" I asked when she returned several minutes later.

"Mom, I don't know what you are talking about. There wasn't anyone else in the bathroom. Just me."

"Oh!" I exclaimed. "She must have left in a hurry just after I did. It was very strange the way she kept watching me. What did you think about the little window between the bathroom stalls? I've never seen anything like that before. It was embarrassing because I could see her watching me. Can you imagine someone doing something like that?"

My daughter collapsed in the backseat of the car laughing hysterically. Between her shrieks of laughter and gasps for air, I heard her say, "Mom! That wasn't a window! It was a mirror."

And So, He Does!

I know without any doubt that the Lord's children would never have made it through this day without His mercy. We ran into it at every turn, didn't we? In His unending mercies, He saved us from the worst of the worst that could happen today, and in a hundred different ways, he even saved us from ourselves. Oh, yes! The Lord's mercy is unending. Even when it seemed mercy was not to be found, there He was stretching it forth to each one who came empty-handed, seeking His face. Oh, we are so to be pitied.

But it gives Him great pleasure to love us with His mercy. And so, He does.

I know without any shadow of a doubt that the Lord's children would not have made it through this day without His grace showering down on us. It covered every ugly thing that sprouted up and bore wings to fly into our minds and hearts and out of our mouths. Oh, yes! He gave us grace to think the good thought, to love the unlovable, and to say the thing that would lift up and encourage, not cast down and destroy. His grace in our hearts wrestles against every evil imagination as it rises proud and belligerent to bring us harm and Him dishonor. Yes, that grace, that unspeakable gift, saved us in a hundred different ways today. He even saved us from ourselves as we trusted Him with those things that torment our thoughts, those things that hammer away to weaken our resolve to follow Him. We are weary, but His grace is deep and sweet—a well that refreshes.

Oh, friends! It gives Him great pleasure to love us through His grace. And so, He does.

I know without the least inkling of doubt that the Lord's children would not have made it through this day without His love filling us up. It was in a hundred different ways today that He showed us how much He loves us, and it gave Him great pleasure to show up at every turn to bless us with His presence. We thought we were alone in our sorrow, drowning in our despair, but there He was to rescue us just as we were on the brink of disaster. The world emptied our cups, but He filled us up full to overflowing! His love is sweet as it rushes over us, filling in the cracks of bitter disappointment. It is a healing balm, and we can close our eyes to rest, knowing that we are made according to His good pleasure and for His praise and glory.

Dearly beloved, it gives Him great pleasure to love us. And so, He does.

"Mercy unto you, and peace, and love, be multiplied" (Jude 1:2).

Move Over, Sodom ...
You've Got Company!

As a pastor's wife, I've listened to a lot of sermons over the years. I received Christ in February 1980, and I can't even begin to imagine how many sermons I've heard since then. It's been my pleasure and such an honor to sit under my husband's teaching for the past thirty-seven years. But one of the best blessings of being in ministry is all of the wonderful men of God that the Lord has used to grow me *up* in Him—preachers such as Tom Casady, L. D. Sowder, Rick Patterson, Jerry Francisco, Rick Wadley, Tom Muskrat, Jack Sanders, and more recently, Malcolm Burleigh. I thank God for their faithfulness in preaching the truth of the Word. I thank Him for their availability to speak truth into my life, and I'm so very grateful that the Lord has blessed me with a teachable spirit that longs to learn more about Him. I long to know Him, and I love to sit at the beautiful feet of those who are called to preach the Word.

One of the godliest couples of all time is Billy and Ruth Graham. Their ministry has spanned decades, reaching millions of people with the Word of God. He has been blessed with such a wonderful gift of preaching the truth and simplicity of the gospel so that all may hear and understand. However, I only have on small little quibble with something his wife once said. (Is that allowed?)

It's reported that several years ago Ruth made the statement that if God doesn't judge America, He'll have to apologize to Sodom and Gomorrah.[9] I understand the gist of what she said and Billy often repeated over the years. I understand the point they were trying to make. But, at the same time, I understand that the rain falls on the just and the unjust. God is sovereign, and He doesn't ever have to *apologize* for being justified in His judgments or actions! He's God!

Have you seen the bumper sticker that reads, "God said it. I believe it. That settles it."? I cringe in my spirit every time I see that! Listen, friend, God said it. That settles it. Period! Whether I believe it or not, God's Word is forever settled and established in heaven! (Psalm 119:89) He doesn't need for me to agree with Him for His Word to be truth! "God said it. That settles it!"

Many times do we hear of our dear country, the United States of America, being compared to Sodom and Gomorrah. In fact, all you have to do is watch an evening of television to feel like you might be living there. Sodom and Gomorrah are well known for their sexually perverted sin, and they forever will be throughout all generations of mankind. Rightly so! Their judgment serves as a warning to us that God does and will judge all sin. Their lot in life was to be buried beneath burning sulfur. But did you know that sexual sin was only part of their iniquity? Oh, yes. There's more.

"Behold, this was the iniquity of your sister Sodom: pride, overabundance of food, prosperous ease, and idleness were hers and her daughters'; neither did she strengthen the hand of the poor and needy. And they were haughty and committed abominable offenses before Me; therefore I removed them when I saw it, and I saw fit" (Ezekiel 16:49–50 AMPC).

If you notice, sexual sin, the abominable offenses, were mentioned last! Our list starts out with pride, then overabundance of food, and prosperous ease and idleness, and she didn't lift her hand to help the needy. Pride is the first sin listed. In reality, all of the other sins flow out from it.

Does that sound like America? I think it does. Never before have so many been proud, overweight, at ease, and idle! Just as Sodom and Gomorrah were judged for their sin, so we will be judged for ours. We can't say, "Oh, look at their sin and see how awful it was in the sight of God!" Our sin is the same sin. And our sin grows from the root of pride too.

So, what's to become of us? The scripture tells us that:

- Today is the day of salvation (2 Corinthians 6:2).
- His kindness leads us to repentance (Romans 2:4).
- He is the Father of mercies (2 Corinthians 1:3).

He is the God of second chances. Won't you respond to His love while there's still time? The scripture also tells us that there will come a time when the Spirit of God will no longer strive with people. Believe and receive. Your eternal life depends on it.

"In fact, it says, "The message is very close at hand; it is on your lips and in your heart." And that message is the very message about faith that we preach: If you openly declare that Jesus is Lord and believe in your heart that God raised him from the dead, you will be saved" (Romans 10:8–9 NLT).

"Therefore, [there is] no condemnation (no adjudging guilty of wrong) for those who are in Christ Jesus, who live [and] walk not after the dictates of the flesh, but after the dictates of the Spirit" (Romans 8:1 AMPC).

Thank you, Father, Son, and Holy Spirit!

I Know That I Know That I Know

There are those times when all words fail, and only those hidden deep within your heart will come to mind. Mine have to cross a river of memories stretched out over a period of some fifty and seven years ago. Standing beside my mother reciting my catechism at age six, those very words came rushing back as I sat bedside with her, waiting on God to take her home. Years and time and space don't matter. When the heart needs to remember, it does.

Even now in dark of night and weary bodied, totally undone from the day, I fling the words heavenward, knowing the one who hears and answers inclines His ear to me. I breathe out with weakened voice but strong resolve, "Lord Jesus Christ, Son of God, have mercy on me—for I am a sinner."

And He does. I know that I know that I know—He does. Just as His mercy washed over my mother as He took her frail, failing body and weary spirit home, His mercy washes over me, in me, and through me. I quietly wait for sleep to come. I am kissed by His grace and tucked in with His peace. I know I am loved. I know I am forgiven. I am at peace with God—it is unfettered and runs like a river through my weary soul, quietly lulling me to sleep.

Have a good rest, friend. He hath inclined His ear to you as well. Be blessed with His mercy. Be kissed by His grace. Be tucked in with His peace, and know that you are loved. Know that you are forgiven. Be at peace with God. He is drawing near in dark of night, so there is no reason to fear. He longs to bless you with a peace unfettered. Close your eyes. He neither sleeps nor slumbers so that you can.

"Behold, he that keepeth Israel shall neither slumber nor sleep" (Psalm 121:4).

"Mercy and truth are met together; righteousness and peace have kissed each other" (Psalm 85:10).

Careless Talk Costs Lives

In our world today, millions of dollars are spent every year in advertising. We advertise products, businesses, events, ideas, people, and hundreds and hundreds of other things. We come up with catchy little slogans and songs, hoping to capture the attention of John Q. Public so that we might sell him our wares.

In the 1940s a very unusual advertising campaign was launched nationwide with a catchy little phrase printed on millions of posters, warning Americans to refrain from loose talk. Many of the posters sported a comical drawing of Hitler listening in on unsuspecting gossipers bearing the phrase "Careless Talk Costs Lives." Another one was captioned, "Loose Lips Sink Ships." While it's easy to see the implications of loose talk in the middle of a world war with a madman lurking about, we may fail to see how loose talk can affect us today. But the truth is, this little saying has never been truer![10]

Scripture tells us that:

"He who guards his mouth keeps his life, but he who opens wide his lips comes to ruin" (Proverbs 13:3 AMPC).

"With his mouth the godless man destroys his neighbor ..." (Proverbs 11:9 AMPC).

"Death and life are in the power of the tongue, and they who indulge in it shall eat the fruit of it [for death or life]" (Proverbs 18:21 AMPC).

The scripture is very clear. We ought to avoid careless talk and watch what we advertise! Many people today, even in Christian circles, are harboring the sins of gossip and abuse. The tongue is being used as a weapon to destroy reputations, character, self-esteem, and respect.

We read in James 3:8–11:

> "But the tongue can no man tame; it is an unruly evil, full of deadly poison. Therewith bless we God, even the Father; and therewith curse we men, which are made after the similitude of God. Out of the same mouth proceedeth blessing and cursing. My brethren, these things ought not so to be. Doth a fountain send forth at the same place sweet water and bitter?"

It is truth. God is calling us to a deeper love walk with Him and with one another. But our love will never be deep and our walk will never be close if we are failing in this discipline of the mouth! Beloved, let's ask God to set a guard before our mouths and to keep watch at the door of our lips!

Please, Lord! You know how we struggle with this. Help us to only say things that are pleasing in Your hearing—words that will bring honor to You. Help us to follow Your lead and walk in the way of love.

Are You a Maze or Amazed?

Good morning! Got plans? Is your day mapped out? Your week? Your month? Your year? Your life?

I love to plan! I love to be organized and make my lists. After all, we are told in the scripture to "let all things be done decently and in order" (2 Corinthians 14:40). I fervently work to make my lists and then I make a list of my lists. But no matter how hard I try to stick to the list, my plans are changed, my day is interrupted, and things don't flow. Sometimes it's as if I run into a brick wall, and I am stopped dead in my tracks. Looking back on my day, I discover that my well-laid plans have turned into a maze of problems, situations, trials, and tribulations. Many are the days that I don't seem to accomplish one thing on my list of things to do. Before I know it, my list grows longer and longer.

When I was a child, I loved playing with maze games. You know, the little puzzles that you hold in your hand. The object of the game is to see how long it takes you to get the little ball from a starting point on the outer circle to the innermost circle. Sometimes it would seem that every path was blocked, and no matter which way I sent that little ball rolling, it would encounter a dead end. Just like my best-laid plans! How frustrating that is to a person who is so planned, so organized, so in control of scheduling, and pleased with routine.

The evil one loves to mess up our plans. Sometimes he uses other people to create the maze in our lives. Sometimes he uses the telephone, lack of electricity, traffic jams, poor health, bad attitudes, heavy burdens, or even the weather to create those brick walls in our lives. Not that he has total control over any of those things, but he sure uses them to discourage us, weigh us down, and interrupt our plans. We forget to walk in the Spirit of God. Instead, we walk and respond to everything in the flesh. We let the least little thing control our emotions, our actions, and our spirits. He, Satan, works in our flesh, also known as the "old man," the "old nature." He loves it when our old nature wars against the new nature, the new man.

The scripture says that "all things work together for the good of those who love God and are called according to His purpose" (Romans 8:28). So, we know that no matter what interruptions take place in our day, it is God's plan that those interruptions should be opportunities. Opportunities for ministry, opportunities for bringing glory to His holy name, opportunities for introducing someone to the Son of God, whose Spirit lives in our hearts.

Proverbs 3:6 AMPC states, "In all your ways know, recognize and acknowledge Him and He will direct and make straight and plain your paths."

Wow! Straight paths! I love that!

Here's another one, Isaiah 30:21 AMPC: "And your ears will hear a word behind you saying, 'This is the way; walk in it, when you turn to the right hand and when you turn to the left.'"

Thank you, Lord! A straight path and a voice to guide me!

"Your word is a lamp to my feet and a light to my path" (Psalm 119:105 AMPC).

Let's don't stop now!

"Concerning the works of men, by the word of Your lips I have avoided the ways of the violent (the paths of the destroyer). My steps have held closely to Your paths [to the tracks of the one who has gone on before]; my feet have not slipped" (Psalm 17:4–5 AMPC).

Beloved, when your plans are a maze, don't keep your eye on the ball, and certainly don't look at that big wall! Keep your eyes on the Lord Jesus Christ. He will direct your steps, keep your paths straight, and tell you which way to go. He may not deliver you *out of* the maze, but He will always deliver you *through* it!

He is so amazing! "Amazing grace how sweet the sound that saved a wretch like me. I once was lost, but now I'm found, was blind, but now I see!"[11]

Got plans? Give them to our amazing Jesus, and watch what He does with your day, your week, your life!

Do You Want to Know a Secret?

Ah, what a silly question that is! Everybody loves a secret! The only problem is that everyone loves a secret so much that by the time they get around to sharing it with three or four others, it's no longer a secret … everyone *knows*. Even the Beatles crooned a tune back in the early sixties asking that all-time probing question, "Do you want to know a secret?"[12]

When our daughter, Jené, was a little girl, she thought it was okay to tell secrets as long as you whispered. So, a night of bunking out with the girls from the youth group at church would often result in gales of laughter and squeals of denial the next morning as she shared teenage secrets with her daddy-pastor and me.

Did you know that some of the greatest secrets ever told are right at our fingertips? Flip through your Bible to find this verse: "The secret things belong unto the LORD our God, but the things which are revealed belong to us and to our children forever, that we may do all the words of this law" (Deuteronomy 29:29).

God's Word is full of secrets! And while there are some secrets He has not shared with us, things that are known only to Him, He has revealed to us those things that are profitable to us concerning salvation, how to live a godly life in Christ Jesus, what we are to be doing until He comes again … and on and on the list goes. He has revealed so much to us that we can read and study the Bible our whole lives and never come to the end of all He has given to us.

Now, I'm not much interested in the secrets that have to be whispered around the water cooler or church vestibule, but I am interested in the secrets of God. The more I read those things He has revealed, the more I understand how to apply them to my life and share them with others. I love that about God! It is okay to tell His secrets … and we don't have to whisper.

When we lie down to that time of blessed sleep, may we rest well in Him and wait quietly while He teaches us in the night seasons.

> "I will bless the Lord who has given me counsel; my heart also instructs me in the night seasons. I have set the Lord always before me; because *He is* at my right hand I shall not be moved. Therefore my heart is glad, and my glory rejoices; my flesh also will rest in hope. For You will not leave my soul in Sheol, Nor will You allow Your Holy One to see corruption. You will show me the path of life; in Your presence *is* fullness of joy; at Your right hand *are* pleasures forevermore" (Psalm 16:7–11 NKJV).

Guard My Mouth, Lord!

When I was a young child, I was backward and so shy. I could spend hours just staring off into space saying nothing. There were many times that I thought I would like to be a cloistered nun, shut away with prayers and penance, left to solitude and conversation with God. Interestingly enough, I was born tongue-tied and at a very young age had a bit of surgery to correct the defect. A tightly bound tongue being loosed and gaining freedom, only to be silenced by my backward ways and shyness—such irony.

At times I find myself in that position now, living a very quiet life in a funeral home, doing those last things for the dead, shut away with my thoughts and with my God, enduring the silence for this season. I am often tongue-tied with grieving family members who express their dismay in a variety of ways—some giving in to anger, others fits of weeping. There really is nothing to say at those times. I give comfort with appropriately placed boxes of tissues, candy dishes full of mints, soft steps on the carpet, and prayers.

Over the years I've made up for those long periods of silence as a child, coming to my own in a sort of fashion, and taking on the life of a chatter bug. Words have become my life. I love both writing them and speaking them, realizing that I am accountable to God for every idle word spoken. I am conscious of making my words count for something, mainly for God. There's nothing I enjoy more than teaching from God's Word, some nugget of buried treasure being revealed and voiced to those who are hungry to know Him.

I do love to write, turning a word or twisting a phrase to make a hard heart crumble and eyes that never cry wet with tears. I love to voice some truth from His Word so that he who hath ears to hear may hear. For those whose ears are deaf and hear not a word, it is my pleasure and honor to form words with my fingers, hands, and expression of face that they too may hear the truth with their eyes and know Him.

I'm sure I've made up for those many times that I had nothing to say by saying too much. I love to joke and tease, laugh and carry on. I have a happy heart that seems to spill out when my mouth is opened, and although I can't sing, it would seem as if my laughter and voice are songs that fill the air with melody and joy. I thank God that when He gave me my voice, He gave me a garland for my ashes, the oil of joy for my mourning, and the garment of praise for my spirit of heaviness. More than any other, His Word has transformed my heart and life.

Several years ago, I was involved in a conversation with friends. There was teasing and laughter as we enjoyed dinner and fellowship together. Sometimes I have a wit that is a bit too quick, and while it might be fun and funny, it doesn't bring honor to God. I have a bit of sarcasm and self-deprecating humor that seem to encourage laughter in a way that isn't becoming. I'm often filled with regret over having said too much. This particular night after such an outburst of laughter and fun, someone said, "Oh! That Qené—she'll say anything!" I was instantly filled with remorse and shame. If I could have bitten my tongue out, I would have done so. I resolved that very night not to be the type of person that will just say anything. I want to say those things that will encourage and uplift others and bring honor to God. There's nothing wrong with laughter and fun conversation, but dripping sarcasm and sharp wit that wounds others or seems crass and ungodly should have no place in my mouth, as Christ has asked me to carry a good witness for Him.

My husband always says, "Whatever is in the well of the heart comes out through the bucket of the mouth." I love the way that Jesus said it best:"A good man out of the good treasure of his heart bringeth forth that which is good, and an evil man out of the evil treasure of his heart bringeth forth that which is evil: for out of the abundance of the heart his mouth speaketh" (Luke 6:45).

For many years now, my personal prayer has been: "Teach me good judgment, wise and right discernment and knowledge, for I have believed (trusted, relied on, and clung to) your commandments" (Psalm 119:66 AMPC).

I know that good judgment, wise and right discernment, and knowledge all come from Him. The nearer I draw to Him, He leads me to pray …

"Set a watch, O LORD, before my mouth; keep the door of my lips" (Psalm 141:3).

One of Those Days

Oh, we all have our days, don't we? You, know those days. Days when you think there is more hair in the sink and your brush than there is on your head. Days when you follow your lip line very carefully with your favorite lipstick and then you realize you just painted a thin straight line across the middle of your face.

You know those days. Days when the elastic snaps in the waistline of your britches and in horror you discover they still stay up. Days when you call one of your children or grand-ones every name in the family except his own. Those days when you want to turn back the clock to that year, that day, that moment when your "Wow!" turned into "Whoa!"

You know those days? Yeah, me neither. Ha!

Friends, there's gonna be those days, but God has every hair on our heads numbered. He has every tear we shed in a bottle. And He has every desperate prayer that we've ever flung up to the heavens gathered in a bowl.

Oh, yes, there will be days like that, but our God loves us dearly and gives us strength for each day.

He is the strength of our life. "My flesh and my heart faileth: *but* God *is* the strength of my heart, and my portion forever" (Psalm 73:26).

The joy of the Lord is our strength! "Then he said unto them, Go your way, eat the fat, and drink the sweet, and send portions unto them for whom nothing is prepared: for *this* day *is* holy unto our Lord: neither be ye sorry; for the joy of the LORD is your strength" (Nehemiah 8:10).

Have a joyful heart today, friends. And remember, if you need a safety pin for your britches or a pretty lipstick to paint on a smile, I can help you out.

The God Bless Yous

You've seen them. I know you have! Perhaps you don't have to look far to see them, at least no further than the end of your nose, because this time of the year you experience them too. You know how it starts. Scratchy throat; itchy, watery, red eyes; a runny nose; continuous sneezing; crankiness from loss of sleep, and sheer frustration from all those symptoms that are suddenly out of control.

We call them allergies. Children sometimes call them the "Aaaaachhh-Choooos," but my grand-ones call them the "God Bless Yous."

The sneezing can be the worst. People who frequently sneeze two or three times, suddenly sneeze dozens of times. Aaah-choo; aaaahh-choo; aaaahhhh-chooo! And on and on it goes!

This time of the year, the culprit causing these symptoms is pollen or mold that invades our air space and is breathed into our bodies triggering an allergic reaction to this foreign substance. The symptoms indicate something is wrong. Something is in our bodies that's not supposed to be there.

Just as that is a physical reaction, there's also a spiritual application that takes place when something that's not supposed to be there enters our hearts. The symptoms are different, but you know they are there, and they possibly include no desire for Bible reading and prayer, lack of church attendance, a cranky spirit, a judgmental attitude, no love, no joy, and no peace. Sound familiar?

What is the culprit that is creating this host of symptoms? Sin. Something that is not pleasing to God has entered the life of the believer, and it's a miserable feeling! Let me say that again: it's a *miserable* feeling. It's worse than a case of the "Aaaaahhhhh-Choooos"!

For nasal allergies, the remedy is an antihistamine. For sin? The remedy is simple and a relatively easy pill to swallow.

"If we confess our sins, He is faithful and just to forgive our sins, and purify us from all unrighteousness" (1 John 1:9).

Oh! And "God bless you!"

Two words are my very favorite of all. They are two words that I search for when I'm reading my Bible—two words that make all the difference in the world to you and me. Two words that at the end of this very long day, we need to remember: "But God ..."

Here is an example of one that we particularly need to hear today. It's one that will restore our peace and calm our spirits:

- "My flesh and my heart fail, *but God* is the strength of my heart and my portion forever" (Psalm 73:26 NIV; emphasis mine).

This one is mind-boggling to me, and the gratitude I feel when I read it is immeasurable! How about you?

- "For when we were yet without strength, in due time Christ died for the ungodly. For scarcely for a righteous man will one die: yet peradventure for a good man some would even dare to die. *But God* commendeth his love toward us, in that, while we were yet sinners, Christ died for us" (Romans 5:6–8; emphasis mine).

I love this "but God!" It fills me with hope and great expectancy. It reminds me that God loves us so very much, and one day there will be no more suffering, no tears, no pain, no loss, no death.

- "But as it is written: "Eye has not seen, nor ear heard, nor have entered into the heart of man the things which God has prepared for those who love Him." *But God* has revealed *them* to us through His Spirit. For the Spirit searches all things, yes, the deep things of God" (1 Corinthians 2:9–10; emphasis mine).

If you are feeling hopeless and defeated, take a journey through the scriptures and look for the "but God ..." statements. Your strength will be renewed, your peace will flow unfettered like a river, your heart will swell with thanksgiving, and your spirit will dance with joy!

Let's remember one another in prayer for blessings of God's strength and courage, His peace, and healing mercies. Yes, life is hard, but God is good.

"Give thanks to the LORD, for he is good! His faithful love endures forever" (Psalm 136:1 NLT).

Until He Comes

I'm one of those people who likes to have a plan! Even though I haven't had children living in my home for several years, I love the routine of the school year, and I'm always so relieved when school gets back into full swing. I don't like it when people or things mess with the rhythm of my life!

As a person who likes to have a plan of action, I love lists! I'm sure you've heard of people like me ... and possibly even laughed at people like me ... but I'm one of those people who make lists of their lists! I'm more productive with a list. I'm more efficient and accountable for my time when I have a list and stick to it. I like knowing what's going to happen and when.

During the past thirty-seven years of ministry, God has had to work with me and on me about this. He's had to show me that what I view as an interruption is really an opportunity—an opportunity for ministry. It has been hard for me to turn loose of my lists and go with the flow. His flow! But I'm doing better than I used to, just not as good as I should in remembering this. Thankfully, His Holy Spirit is the great convictor, and He jabs an elbow in my spiritual ribs when I forget to be available and flexible for opportunities to minister.

I've discovered many times in the scriptures that God loves lists too! They're everywhere in the Word, and I'm convinced He put them there for people like me! I just do better when I know what to expect. I was so excited when I found a wonderful list of things to do until the Lord comes! Even if you're not a list maker, don't you want to know what He wants you to do until He comes? I thought so. Take a look at this:

> But the end and culmination of all things have now come near; keep sound minded and self-restrained and alert, therefore [for the practice of] prayer. Above all things have intense and unfailing love for one another, for love covers a multitude of sins [forgives and disregards the offenses of others.] Practice hospitality to one another (those of the household of faith.) [Be hospitable, be a lover of strangers, with brotherly affection for the unknown guests, the foreigners, the poor, and all others who come your way who are of Christ's body.] And [in each instance] do it ungrudgingly (cordially and graciously, without complaining but as representing Him.) As each of you has received a gift (a particular spiritual talent, a gracious divine endowment,) employ it for one another as [befits] good trustees of God's many-sided grace [faithful stewards of the extremely diverse powers and gifts granted to Christians by unmerited favor.] Whoever speaks, [let him do it as one who utters] oracles of God; whoever renders service, [let him do it] as with the strength which God furnishes abundantly, so that in all things God may be glorified through Jesus Christ (the Messiah.) To Him be the glory and dominion forever and ever (through endless ages.) Amen (so be it) (1 Peter 4:7–11 AMPC).

Here's our list of things to do until Jesus comes!

1. Be sober (sound minded in doctrine). This will require reading and studying the Word of God.

2. Exhibit the fruit of self-control.
3. Be alert and consistent in our prayers (public and private).
4. *Love* one another!
5. Forgive and disregard the offenses of others.
6. Be hospitable to the household of faith, the stranger, and the poor.
7. Don't complain or have a complaining spirit about serving others.
8. Remember you are His representative here on earth.
9. Use your spiritual gifts/talents to bless the saints in the body of Christ.
10. Glorify God in all you say and do.

That should keep us busy and out of trouble! Yes, there's plenty to do until He comes! When I keep this list in mind, it's almost impossible to think of interruptions as anything other than opportunities!

"So be careful how you live. Don't live like fools, but like those who are wise. Make the most of every opportunity in these evil days" (Ephesians 5:15–16 NLT).

P-Prayers

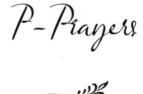

I have a list of P-prayers that I love to pray for friends, family, and myself. They pretty much cover everything we could possibly need at any hour of the day. Maybe you'd like to join your prayers with mine?

When I pray I ask the Lord to bless us all with *His* pardon (Luke 18:13), *His* peace (John 14:27), *His* power (Acts 1:8), *His* provision (Psalm 68:19), *His* protection (2 Thessalonians 3:3), *His* perspective (Philippians 2:5), and *His* perseverance (Luke 22:31–32; 1 Corinthians 15:58).

Pardon for our sin and all of our trespasses.

Peace that flows unfettered by circumstance and fear.

Power from the Holy Spirit of the Lord Jesus Christ.

Provision for everything we need in life and ministry—may it be abundant and timely.

Protection from the evil one, who stalks about like a roaring lion, seeking out those whom he may devour. Protection from illness, injury, and harm of every kind.

Perspective from Your point of view, Father! Ours is so skewed by the ways of the world. Help us see people and situations with a supernatural perspective—Yours, Lord! Please reveal the *truth* and expose all *lies*.

Perseverance to help us to be strong and not faint in the way. When we are weak, please ... You be strong in us. Be our wisdom and our confidence as we fight the good fight and finish our course.

Trust Him, friends. P-prayers will see you through a dark night of the soul.

Something of a Miracle

Some of the miracles in my life are of the handmade kind. Having no skill with needles or thread, scissors, paint, or glue – I discovered that I enjoy crocheting. Taught under the watchful eye of a right-handed mother and a left-handed mother-in-law, I eventually learned how to control the tension of the yarn. At first I just couldn't get it. Everything I made came out in a little ball or in the shape of a cup with the edges curled – unbending even under the pressure of a steam iron. My mom was able to show me a pattern though, and once I finally got the tension under control I enjoyed making afghans for my family and friends.

I enjoy giving people something I've made. They always seem so impressed that the blankets lay flat and the pattern is so exact. I love the pattern. It is a ripple stitch, and right from the start I'm able to tell if I've made a mistake. The pattern just won't let me get off track. I do have to admit though, while people are oohing and ahing over my handmade miracle a little voice deep within badgers me, "Tell them! Tell them now! Tell them what a rotten knot-maker you are and that you can't be held responsible if something goes wrong in the spin cycle when the miracle is washed!"

But, of course, I say nothing. I smile, I accept their praise, and I hope that before that fateful wash day comes, the Lord will have called me home, and even a pile of yarn tangled and twisted around the machine agitator will seem precious in my absence.

My sister knows me. When I give her the blanket I've made for her God-made miracle by the name of Kelsey April, she'll understand. It's such a sweet little blanket for such a sweet little baby – all one pound, twelve ounces of her! Every stitch was made with my heart and mind on my sister and her new little daughter who was born at 27 weeks … praying for her, loving her, and thanking God that He used doctors and nurses to nurture and care for this littlest angel.

Yes, my sister will understand about my knots. I'll be able to tell her. In fact, she'll understand so well that I have visions of my great-great-great-great niece presenting her own daughter with this time-worn, handmade miracle, saying, "This little blanket has been in our family for over 100 years and it's never been washed!"

This handmade miracle of mine reminds me of my spiritual life. I'm a miracle. I'm made in the image of God, born again by His Holy Spirit, living a life that follows a pattern designed by Him. A pattern that will bring Him glory. I always know when I've strayed off the pattern God has set before me for my life. His still small voice shouts within my soul, telling me to shape up, get it right, and try again. His love and patience draw me back to the pattern.

And, I'm washed! I'm cleansed by His blood, never falling apart in the spin cycle of this world. God's own Word tells me that I am His workmanship created in Christ Jesus for good works which God prepared beforehand that I should walk in them. (Ephesians 2:10) My life, a miracle of the God-made kind, is continually being worked on, improved and completed. Philippians 1:6 says, "Being confident of this very thing, that He who has begun a good work in you will complete it until the day of Jesus Christ." That's good news for me – He is still working on me. But, there will be a day, the day of Jesus Christ, when it is all said and done. At that great and wonderful day, I want my life to have been one of love, prayer, praise, and unfettered peace – a life that has shown glory to God through His workmanship, for He is truly worthy to be praised.

Abba, Father, I thank You for the work You have done in my life, washing me in your blood, saving me by Your grace, and keeping me through Your Holy Spirit. Please God, watch over Your littlest angel, Kelsey April, and continue Your work in her life that she might bring glory to Your name, and that her life might be evidence of Your love. I pray for my sister, Marni. Oh God, don't let her get caught in the spin cycle of this world without You! Keep her nerves from unraveling and fill her with Your peace. Amen.

God's Goodness Is Toward Me

God has been so good to us today, I think I'll stay awake a while longer to enjoy it. We awoke this morning to the blessing of life and good health. The minute our feet hit the floor, we were walking in the light of His love, and there was no place our feet trod that we were able to step out of that light. There was no moment all throughout this day when we were without His love.

There might have been moments when the fear and anxiety of this life could have overwhelmed us, but we continue to clutch tightly to the truth of His Word. The Word spoken by Christ has made its home in our hearts and minds. The lies of this world, or even those of my own heart, cannot stand in the presence of the truth of His Word. It is forever established in heaven, and we walk confidently with our lives anchored in His Word.

My own strength was so weak today! If not for the strength of His Spirit, I could do nothing. But He makes me strong, and when His eyes search for those whose heart totally belongs to Him, He shows Himself stronger still in me. His Spirit gives me discernment and wisdom as I walk in the light of His love, clutching tightly to the truth of His Word, waiting for the Lord Himself to give me direction. All the while, He lavishes me with His good favor, and I drink it in deeply, giving Him praise because He is so worthy of glory, honor, and praise.

His promises delight my soul and bring me great comfort through the day. I remember them, I quote them, I believe them, and I anxiously wait for that day when all will come to pass. He is our hope. He is our only hope.

Thank You, Lord, for the blessing of this life. Oh, yes! We have a trial or two, You know we do. But You teach us how to walk in grace as well as love, in mercy as well as strength, and in peace as well as hope. Thank You for your watch-care, Lord. You were so good to us today. You've seen us through to the very end of it.

I only ask that Your blessings continue as You tuck me in with peace, power, protection, and provision. I will sleep in sweet rest tonight as You have continually been with me. Please, just spend the night and keep watch over me as I rest. I'll never make it without You, Lord.

None of us will ever make it through without You.

The Number of My Days

From the very first day that I found out what happened to me, my heart has been exploding with joy to be alive. Early on in my recovery from a near-death illness, I determined in my heart that I would not waste my suffering. Since then, I look for every opportunity to tell people about what Jesus did for me. Even to this day, it makes me weep when I tell it—deep, heaving tears of thanksgiving and joy.

In the scripture we read, "But you must not forget this one thing, dear friends: A day is like a thousand years to the Lord, and a thousand years is like a day" (2 Peter 3:8 NLT).

That's much the way it was for me during my illness—my near-death experience. For me, the period from March 11 through March 31 was all one day. And every day for the next two months of rehabilitation would be as a thousand years.

I'm not certain what day it was when I first realized and understood that I was ill with type A influenza, double pneumonia, severe acute respiratory distress syndrome, and sepsis, but I told my family that I was shocked to hear that news as I was certain that I had been kidnapped. That statement provided a few moments of humor in an otherwise very stressful situation. But it was true.

I was heavily sedated, in a coma-like state, during these events and only conscious during times when the doctors eased up on the drugs to see if I could breathe on my own, so for most of this story, I will be telling it from my family's perspective and my perception.

Simply said, perspective is a point of view based on reality, but perception is an individual's interpretation of things. It is an understanding a person gains through awareness.[13] As we go through the story, you will see that there is a huge difference between the reality of my illness and my perception, which was based on my experience and interpretation of all that I saw and heard. My perception was also based on a spiritual perspective—something that is only experienced standing with Jesus at the door to death discussing your future.

It seems a strange thing to lose time, but that's what happened to me. It's almost as if the whole month of March didn't happen. I only have little glimpses of memory, but nothing of significance that would tie all the pieces of this crazy puzzle together.

For instance, I have no memory of being at work on March 11, but I did work that day; in fact, I had a very busy day with dozens of e-mails, phone calls, and letters. My coworkers tell me I was excited and bubbly for the weekend. I had a good day, a happy day, and I even got off work a little early, which is always great on a Friday.

My Pat said that we stopped at a flea market in Springfield before heading home. It's something we both enjoy, and we've spent many weekends scrounging around dusty shelves looking for items that remind us of family and friends long gone. We only made it down three aisles when I told him I needed to go home because I wasn't feeling well. He asked if I wanted to stop for dinner on the way, and I said, "No, I need to go home. I need to go home now." I have no memory of that, but he later showed me a plate that we bought at the flea market. I do remember the plate, but not that we bought it shopping that day.

During the course of my recovery, my family told me of the many of the things that happened to me during those lost weeks. Sometimes the story feels vaguely familiar. Though, at this point in time, I'm not sure if I really remember it or if it's just familiar because we talk about it so often. The one evidence I do have that I was sick and fully aware of that fact is a series of text messages I sent to my director, Malcolm, telling him I wouldn't be able to come into work because I was sick.

On Sunday, March 13, I sent this note, "Do you remember that pesky little cough I had Friday? It turned into monster-flu. I am so pitifully sick; I could use a prayer." He replied, "We are praying for you, Q."

Then, on Monday, March 14, I sent a note saying, "I'm sorry I'm going to miss work today. I'm really sick with the flu." Malcolm replied, telling me to stay home as long as I needed.

On Tuesday, March 15, Malcolm sent me an early morning note asking how I was doing and urging me to stay home again. I replied, "I really, really want to come. But it would be a mistake. I haven't been out of bed for any longer than thirty minutes each day, and I haven't eaten since lunch on Friday. I still have an excruciating headache and a cough that will wake the dead. I'm so pitiful. Brandon is going to listen to my lungs to make sure I don't have pneumonia. I don't think I do. And my hair hurts really, really bad."

On Wednesday, things took a turn for the worse. Late that morning my Pat tried texting me on my phone, messaging me on Facebook, and finally calling me on my cell phone. I'd had a very restless night, and he noticed that my breathing was fast and shallow, so he became worried when he couldn't get ahold of me. It was unusual for him not to be able to reach me, as I always respond quickly to his e-mails and texts. Rushing home in the middle of the day, he contacted our daughter, and she arrived at the house about the same time, finding me confused and in a daze trying to figure out how to work my blood sugar monitor. I looked up and said, "What is this? I don't know what to do with it."

Pat and Jené spent several minutes trying to talk me into going to the doctor, but I didn't want to go. I told them I was too sick to go. Our son-in-law, Brandon, called Jené and she filled him in on what was happening. He said, "Tell your mother to put her sweater on and go to urgent care or I'm calling an ambulance." When she hung up the phone, Jené shoved my arms into a sweater and told her dad to get the key—we were going to see a doctor.

About noon, Malcolm sent me a message asking how I was feeling. My reply came early in the evening, and I said, "I've had a pretty rough day. Heading home after getting a bag of fluids and antibiotics. Thanks for your prayers."

The doctor asked Pat to bring me back into the office on Thursday morning. When we arrived, they immediately took me back to a room. The nurse's aide took my vital signs and was concerned that she wasn't getting it right, so she called for the RN to come in and help. My blood pressure was 73/37. She looked at Pat and said, "I'm calling an ambulance to take her to the emergency room." They kept me in the ER for five hours getting my blood pressure stabilized, giving me IV fluids, and taking several lung x-rays. My temp was 102.7, which is pretty high for someone who normally has a 97.2 body temp. Later that day I was admitted to the Intensive Care Unit. My chest x-rays looked bad and proved I had double pneumonia. A painful swab inserted high into my nasal cavity proved I had type A influenza. Over the course of the next three days, my condition progressed to a very dangerous state as I developed severe acute respiratory distress syndrome and finally sepsis. There was no air moving in my lungs. One hundred percent oxygen was not enough to keep me alive, and there was no choice but to put me on the ventilator.

My daughter tells me that I was very swollen, and my skin coloring looked bad. I had the look of death on my face and in my eyes. My hands were so swollen that my fingers looked like little sausages, and they were purple. Pat and the kids took turns rubbing my arms to comfort me and rubbing my hand trying to lessen the swelling.

My sister Canera, who is a nurse and lives in Connecticut, arrived late that evening. My lips and my extremities were so blue, she was certain I wasn't going to make it. Pat didn't tell me she was coming, but he said when she walked into the room I started crying because I was so glad to see her. She says my first words to her were, "Finally! Somebody is here who knows what she's doing!" My brother also came to visit that night. When he left, he called my sister Marni in Arizona very upset that I was dying.

Sometime that evening one of the nurses told me that it was time to put me on the vent because I was dying and something had to be done. My husband said I refused. I'm sure it's because my mother was a nurse, and I remember her saying when I was a young girl that she'd never seen anyone put on a vent who made it home. Of course, I wanted to go home more than anything, so I said no. Brad, my nurse, said, "Qené? Don't you want me to save your life? You are dying, and we have to do this to help you. It is our one hope for you." I replied, "Yes, please. Save my life."

So, one week after I became ill, I was placed on the ventilator and a feeding tube. My sister René arrived that day. It seemed certain that as my family and friends gathered in the waiting room, there was much to pray about and many fears to be comforted.

Even on the ventilator, my lungs continued to fail. One of the doctors in ICU is a very skilled physician and the only one in our area to use a procedure called proning, in which a patient is placed face down on the bed for sixteen hours at a time while on the vent. The proning helps expand or flatten out the lungs allowing more air flow. Over the course of the next four days, I was flipped three times. Each time, my family watched with dismay, and they were filled with despair that I was going to die. It was hard for them to see me that way, and they began discussing the possibility that our son Woodi would have to be called home from Afghanistan to be with his dad, brother, and sister while they watched my body slowly die. It appeared that their one last hope was not going to work for me.

If I have any memory of that lost time, it is that I felt my life slipping away from this existence into the next with God. It is during this time that I saw Jesus standing at my side, and I asked Him, "Is this to be the number of my days?"

I felt my life slipping away into the night, light and life leaving body and soul. It seemed certain that I would die—die to this life, but alive in the next with Christ. I could feel the enormity of my Pat's grief fill my soul with despair. I knew he thought I was going to die, and his grief was deep, consuming, and heavy, like a cloak wrapped about my dying frame. His grief became mine. I heard the heart-cry of mourning in my children and grand-ones. I longed to be with them and comfort them. They lovingly cared for me and spoke gentle reassurances of love. But there was that day or two that in my spirit I heard the mourning of their hearts.

There I was. I was alone, so very alone with God. I slowly opened my eyes to see Him standing by my bedside. When I saw Him, my heart was filled with praise and my eyes were filled with tears. What a sight to behold! Our precious Savior, our Jesus! Looking back at this experience, the miracle lies not in the fact that I saw Him, but that He saw me! The one who created heaven and earth, the one who can hold the stars in the palm of His hand, the one who knows the depth of the deepest sea. He saw me. He saw a sixty-one-year-old grandmother on her bed of death. I cried out for Him, and He showed up for me.

His precious and powerful peace filled my room, completely enveloping the whole of it, calming my anxious thoughts, giving me confidence that in life as well as death, nothing was going to happen to me that was out of His holy realm. Such power in His presence, such peace!

Who could ever know that, except those standing at the door to death with Jesus by their side? I cared not about His appearance. I cannot give you a description of what I saw. I was so overcome with the power of His presence.

I had only one question. Only one thought I dared to speak. "Oh, Lord! Is this to be the number of my days?"

Strong and powerful, quiet and loving, He responded. "Qené, whether it is or whether it isn't, you are mine, and I will never leave you nor forsake you."

I didn't walk through the door that night, though I would be given a second chance in another dark night of the soul. But I came away both times with the assurance that God has something else for me to do, and only He would know the number of my days.

There is one thing, one reality that you need to know. At that time of death, it will be just you and God. It will not matter how many people are around your bed, how many people are crying in the waiting room, or how many people across the face of this earth are praying for you—it will be just you and God.

We will each have our appointment with death. This wasn't mine. But I beg you to be ready for yours. Won't you turn your heart to Christ and receive His gift of salvation? There is nothing to fear in death when you know that true life lies on the other side in heaven with Him. The power of His presence is an awesome thing to behold. You can have that presence every moment of every day—in you, around you, on you—but only through Christ. You need to know Him now to live with Him then.

One of my first memories is of waking up being upside down. I have no idea where this fell in the timeline of my illness. I felt very groggy and confused. It was hard for me to think, and I wondered if I had been drugged; it certainly felt that way. I did not feel sick. I did not feel any pain. I was aware of movement around me as if several people were bustling about. I tried to move but could not; it was then I realized that I was bound and had a gag of some sort in my mouth. I could not speak, though I did try. I felt movement similar to a boat rocking in the waves, and I heard weird music that I couldn't identify. It sounded Asian, and the volume kept changing, which made it sound strange and sinister. I did not hear anyone speak to me. Several people would drift in and out of the area I was confined to, but no one spoke. I'm sure this lasted only a moment, and then, wondering where I was and what had happened to me, I closed my eyes once again into a deep sleep.

In the next memory, I am face up in a darkened room, but there is a light beyond the room that filters in through loose curtains that seem to blow with a wind of movement when people pass. The curtains are similar to vertical blinds, though they are not stiff, they are flowing and loose. They are silver on the bottom two-thirds, and the upper third is like mesh allowing light to enter my room from the hallway beyond.

I know I've been drugged and struggle for a moment to think clearly. I am still bound, though I think I can move my hands a little, and I try signing to one of the people nearby. "Where am I? Who are you? Where is Pat?" No one responds. My hands don't move well; they feel stiff and awkward, so I think that they can't understand my signs. I feel paralyzed and bound, unable to move. I still feel the rocking of a boat. I do not recognize anyone that comes in and out or anyone who walks behind the curtain, yet they pause to talk to one another, and I am certain they are talking about me. They are all wearing masks.

What has happened to me? I have no memory of how I got here. I feel frustrated and agitated that I can't find Pat. I wonder, have I been kidnapped? Was Pat kidnapped too? Is he dead? Are my captors going to kill me? Why would they kidnap me? I am aware of human trafficking, but why would anyone kidnap me, an old woman? Does anyone know I'm missing? Is anyone praying for me? I suddenly feel a deep sense of grief and sorrow. It is overwhelming, and I realize it is coming from my Pat. I don't know where he is, but I know he thinks I am going to die. I think so too. I try not to cry or be afraid. I close my eyes, and I ask God to draw near. Please God ... I need your help.

During another period of wakefulness, I become aware of two girls who enter the room. They seem to be working by my head, just out of my sight. I wonder if they are kind, if they have compassionate hearts, and if I can trust them to help me? One approaches just within my sight, and I struggle to speak around the rubber gag that has been placed in my mouth. "Help me." She looks at me and does not speak. She walks away, and I wonder who she is going to tell that I am awake and asking for help.

Soon the other girl comes close, and I try again. "Help me." Again, this one does not speak. She looks at me for several seconds and then she too walks away. I feel such loss and disappointment as she leaves the room.

There is a man who approaches where I am confined. He is not familiar to me. He is wearing a mask. I do not hear the man speak to me, though his gestures indicate that he is talking to someone. I look at him and say, "Please. Pat." There is no response, and he walks away out of my sight. I would find out much later that these two girls were my daughter and daughter-in-law, and the man was my husband, my Pat.

Once again, I feel my life slipping away, and I know I am going to die at the hand of my captors. I am aware for a second time that I am alone with God. I had only a brief moment of fear following those encounters, but God's presence quickly brings me peace. I felt calm. I know I'm loved. I am still asking Him, "Is this to be the number of my days?"

My doctor refused to give up. Each time I failed to improve, he kept saying, "Let's do it again, I'm just not ready to call Woodi home. Let's prone her just one more time." Then on March 23, twelve days after becoming sick, God began to move. In the previous days, many prayers had been uttered, many tears had been shed, many procedures had been tried, but nothing seemed to work. But at 2:00 a.m., my husband awoke in the night crying out for God to save my life. That same night at 2:00 a.m. my director Malcolm Burleigh awoke in the night crying out to God to save my life. At 2:00 a.m., friends Torrie Thompson, Lynn Hager, Debbie Fearnow, others in our church, and several friends on social media were awakened in the night, crying out to God on my behalf, begging Him to please let me live. It was the most critical night of my illness. Though I was in God's presence, on this occasion, I did not see Jesus, and He did not answer my question. He was answering their prayers.

Early the next morning when Pat and my children arrived at the hospital for visiting hours, the doctor sought them out with the news that he was beginning to see a little improvement in my numbers, and he would not prone me again—he would wait to see my progress. With each hour that passed, my body began to respond. Over the course of the next two days, it was determined that God had done a miracle, and I was out of danger.

The doctor began weaning me off the sedation to prepare me for the removal of the vent. Only then would they know for certain if my lungs could work on their own. There was a very real possibility that they would have to reinsert the vent if I could not breathe on my own. Saturday, March 26 at 9:00 a.m., my vent was to be removed—my family was filled with joy and relief that I would live. Though very weak in body and soul, my spirit was alive with the miracle of God's healing in my body.

I was again roused awake. This time to the sound of song that is very familiar to me. Many years ago, my husband was asked to sing this song at a wedding. He hated it, but he loved the couple who asked him to sing it, so he agreed. It was a country tune called "I Swear."

At the wedding he sang it beautifully, but afterward told me he really struggled to get through it. He only made it, he said, "Because I was singing it to you." When I awakened to the sound of this song, I am sure that it's Pat's way of letting me know that I have been found and would soon be released from my captors.

There was a lot of movement in the area that I was confined to. Suddenly, a man in a mask leaned over me, took my hand, and the first voice I remember hearing since this ordeal began says, "Hi Qené. My name is Jared. Me and these two Jeffers boys are going to get you out of here." I drifted off to sleep thinking he is talking about my two nephews. Bruce is an EMT, and Tim is a deputy sheriff. I thanked God for saving my life, and as I fell back to sleep, I was aware of my body being picked up and carried off to safety.

I'm not certain who told me, but somehow I knew that Zollie, our executive director of U.S. Missions where I work, had arranged for a friend of his to come to the hospital the next morning. This friend has a healing ministry, and he would remove the gag from my throat and pray healing over my mind and body. I did not know the extent of my injuries, but I knew my mind needed healing from the drugs, and I thought perhaps there were injuries in my body from being bound and detained. I had flashing memories of being bodily carried to the back of a car, needles being inserted into my body, and horrific pain that I could only imagine came from being raped. The relief and gratitude I felt that my life had been spared was overwhelming. I was anxious for this healer to come pray over me.

A doctor came to examine me. She said, "You're going to be okay. You are out of danger." I fell asleep once again praying and thanking God for His watch-care over my life.

The next morning, I was dozing due to the heavy sedation I'd been under, but I was excitedly waiting for this healer to come into my room and pray for me. I waited and waited. It seemed like he would never come. Did he forget me, or was he too busy to come? It was hard to be patient.

Then, suddenly, I heard him coming. I could hear his heavy footsteps on the stairway, and as he passed other rooms, he would stop to pray for healing over other patients. He had two people with him; people who traveled with him. I heard one of them say, "Remember Qené, she is waiting for you." The healer replied, "Oh, yes! Yes! We can't forget Qené."

The healer and his assistants swept into my room with a rush—the minute they entered, the healer said, "Mrs. Qené, bow your head, please." He went behind me and placed his hand around my neck and one on my back, all the while praying in a deep, powerful voice. It was a thunderous voice, very powerful and confident, very joyous. The room was full of light and life. Suddenly, out of my throat came the rubber gag! I immediately began praising and thanking God! When my family walked into my room just minutes later, I said, "Oh! Thank God! I thought I was going to die!" They replied, "We thought you were going to die too! This is a miracle! God has done a miracle for you and for our family!"

I couldn't stop praising God for His goodness to me. No longer bound and gagged, I began praying and praising and thanking Him. I was so joyous to be alive and back with my family. "Thank you, God, thank you, healer, thank you, Jesus … thank you for rescuing me!" And on and on I prayed and praised, thanking God for saving my life and freeing me from my kidnappers.

In the days that followed, I asked Pat and the kids who the healer was that Zollie sent to me. Each time I asked they all laughed and said, "There was no healer, Mom. It was just the doctor and a nurse." I was embarrassed but insisted that Zollie sent a healer to me, and he had entered my room with his two assistants. But each time I mentioned it, they laughed and said, "No, that's not what happened." At first, I was embarrassed that I had it all wrong, but in recent weeks God has made it clear to me that Zollie sent his friend Jesus to heal me. The healer was Zollie's friend. The healer was Jesus! It was Jesus and His two angels whom He gave charge over me. As Jesus prayed over me—I was healed from my illness, and I would remain off the vent. Thanks be to God. What a miracle that was on Easter weekend! I will bear in my body, until the day I draw my last breath, the healing power of the Lord Jesus Christ and His Holy Spirit.

I was shocked when my family told me the events of the previous weeks of my illness. I have no memory of a sore throat, killer headache, rabid cough, and lack of oxygen. But many of the events they described to me began to make sense—being taken by ambulance, IVs, breathing masks, feeding tube, ventilator, and a catheter. It all began to fit into place, and I asked them over and over again to tell me the story of what a miracle God had performed in my body.

The next two days and nights were very hard for me. My family was limited to the hours they could be with me. It was such a trauma for me to realize that I had not been kidnapped but was truly deathly ill. I still had no memory of becoming ill, and the confinement by my kidnappers was so vivid, so real. The nurses sent my family home. They were exhausted and needed some rest.

I was all alone and in need of someone to stand with me. Someone to stand in the gap and help me in the night. Twice, when the nurses did not answer my call button, I cried out, "Oh, God, please send me Jesus! Send me Jesus to stand in the gap for me." Both times Jesus appeared at my bedside. His presence completely filled the room with His peace. If you had entered the room, you would not have seen Jesus, but He was there for me. I have no doubt that you would have experienced the presence of God. He filled the room with His love and peace, His grace and mercy, His glory and light. There is no fear in His presence, only love.

The second night when He appeared at my bed, I saw Him for a time and then He stepped away. A little later I woke to see two angels standing at my bedside, quietly talking to each other as if they were friends enjoying each other's company. They were bright and shiny. Such a sweet spirit filled my room that I easily rested because He had given His angels charge over me. I knew Jesus had left them with me, to stand guard over my body for protection.

Though I was healed from my illnesses of type A influenza, double pneumonia, severe ARDS, and sepsis, my body was very weak, like that of a newborn baby. I could do nothing for myself. I couldn't sit up, stand, walk, feed myself, nor take care of my personal needs. It was near one week after my healing that I was released to an in-patient rehabilitation hospital. It was the hardest work I've ever done, but diligence and the thousands of prayers that were being said for me paid off. I was released after eight days to go home for out-patient therapies, still in isolation and on voice rest. It would be two months more before I fully returned to my life and my work.

Thank You, Lord! I will never forget what You did for me. I will never forget my family and friends who prayed for me and loved me back to life.

There are three things I believe the Lord would like for you consider as you think about my testimony:

- Everyone will have their last moment with God. Please be ready. Remember, you must know Him now to live with Him then.

- If you are a believer, there is nothing to fear in death. Jesus will walk with you through the valley of the shadow of death. He will be the only one who stands with you at the door of death. He Himself is the door to heaven. No person comes to the Father except by Him.

- If you have not believed in your heart, nor confessed with your mouth the Lord Jesus Christ, you will walk through the valley of the shadow of death alone. It will be a very frightening thing for you to experience. Please, give your heart to Christ today. Today is the day of salvation.

I don't really know how to explain that many of the things that happened to me were supernatural. There is no way to explain the supernatural power of Jesus and His angels. But everywhere I saw Him during my illness there was peace in His presence ... powerful, wonderful, unfettered peace and love, goodness and mercy, as He walked with me through the valley of the shadow of death.

Oh! Surely, God, Your "goodness and mercy shall follow me all the days of my life, and I will dwell in the house of the Lord forever" (Psalm 23:6).

Would you consider these scriptures?

"For God says, 'At just the right time, I heard you. On the day of salvation, I helped you.' Indeed, the 'right time' is now. Today is the day of salvation" (2 Corinthians 6:2 NLT).

"The Lord isn't really being slow about his promise, as some people think. No, he is being patient for your sake. He does not want anyone to be destroyed, but wants everyone to repent" (2 Peter 3:9 NLT).

"Don't you see how wonderfully kind, tolerant, and patient God is with you? Does this mean nothing to you? Can't you see that his kindness is intended to turn you from your sin?" (Romans 2:4 NLT).

The Blue Cross

When our daughter was five years old, our family moved to Southwest City, Missouri. Noni's bedroom was upstairs, seemingly far away from mom and dad for such a little girl. Sometimes she would be afraid at night, but she was too afraid to come downstairs and find us. When we heard her cry out for us, we would always run upstairs with a glass of water and sit by her until she wasn't afraid anymore. One night while I was tucking her in tight, she told me that she was afraid to be in her room alone. The two boys shared a room and "they have somebody."

As I was holding her trying to calm her down for sleep, I noticed we could see out through the cafe curtains. In plain sight was the lighted blue cross of the Full Gospel Church across the street. I said, "Noni-Roo, when you're afraid, just sit up in bed and look out your window at the cross. Look to Jesus and know that He is protecting you! Let your faith be bigger than your fear." It made her feel better, and with a smile on her face, she was able to lie down and go to sleep.

Our little girl would still be afraid occasionally, especially if her brothers were teasing her, but she knew all she had to do was look to the cross and think about Jesus to feel safe.

During a recent and lengthy hospital stay, I was very sick and near death. While I was in a medically induced coma, my family took turns sitting with me, reading scriptures aloud, and praying with me to bring comfort into a very frightening situation. Little Noni, now thirty-some years old, had been very fearful for me all day. That evening as she stood up to leave my room, she walked over to the window above my bed, looked up, and saw a giant blue lighted cross that topped the hospital building. It was right above my bed. Immediately those words that her dad and I had spoken to her so many years ago came flooding back to her mind and heart. Leaning over my bed with a kiss to tuck me in for the night, she said, "Hey, Mom, guess what? There's a big blue cross right outside your window! Look to Jesus; He will protect you. Let your faith be bigger than your fear."

"Just think of Him ..." (Hebrews 12:3 AMPC).

"Let us therefore come boldly unto the throne of grace, that we may obtain mercy, and find grace to help in time of need" (Hebrews 4:16).

I Cried, He Answered

—⁓—

I'm spending a few moments tonight trying to quiet my spirit and an unrelenting cough by just thinking of Him, our Yeshua, our Savior. Everything that is good and righteous is found in Him, and it is good for us to sit in His presence, soaking in His peace at the end of a long hard day.

What is it you need from Him tonight, friend? What is it that you need Him to do for you? I know for a fact that nothing is too big or too hard for Him. He will meet your need at every turn.

In recent days, there have been two occasions that I called out in despair for Him. Both were similar in nature, similar in request, but He met me for my exact needs on those two occasions.

My illness was so severe that I was very near death. I had been very sick for nearly a month, with three weeks in the hospital and a week on a ventilator. It was exhausting for my family. With my life hanging in the balance, they dreaded the hours they were made to leave me in the care of hospital staff. But following a miraculous healing of my lungs at the last hour, my family had been sent away by the nurses so that I could rest, as could they.

It was very dark and lonely in my room, and I was still confused about my circumstances. I cried out for a nurse to come help me. My voice was very hoarse, as it is even now as I'm writing this. No one heard me. No one came. I pressed on the call button, which was within my reach. It took a lot of effort to press that button, I was very weak, but I managed to press it and was so relieved to see the light and hear the call bell. I waited. But still—no one came. I waited and waited. I waited some more. No one came.

With every passing moment I became more agitated, more desperate. I wanted to cry, but I knew that would only increase my coughing, making it very hard for me to breathe through the bulky oxygen mask I was wearing. Why don't they come? Why would they leave me alone for so long?

Aloud in the darkness with my weak, screechy voice, I prayed, "Oh, God! Please help me! I am so alone, and I have so many needs, but no one will come to help me. I need you! There is no one who will stand with me tonight. No one who will stand in the gap for me, none but the Lord Jesus Christ. Oh, God! Would you send Him? Would you send Him to me to stand with me and care for me in my hour of need? I am so thirsty, and I need someone who can help me."

Even as I prayed, I could feel the power of His presence. It rose up to completely fill the room, and it bathed my weary heart. It quieted my desperate cries. I turned to look, and there He was. There He stood by my bed.

"Qené, I will never leave you nor forsake you."

It's hard to describe the power behind His precious, gentle words to me. It's hard to describe how once so desperate, I was now calm and resting in His presence. The one who is the living water responded to my need. He remained by my bedside as I drifted off into a quiet sleep. Waking every few moments, I could feel His presence ever so near, ever so powerful. And I saw him at my bedside, ministering to my every need.

Do you need peace? Oh, yes, Lord! I am full of fear.

"I am the Prince of Peace."

Do you need comfort? Oh, yes, please! I am most miserable!

"I am the God of all comfort."

Do you need healing? Oh, Yeshua … I am desperate for your touch!

"I am the great physician, and it is by my stripes that you are healed."

Do you thirst? Oh, yes, Lord! My lips are dry and cracked, my throat is on fire from coughing!

"I am the living water. He who drinks of Me will never thirst again."

I finally drifted off into a deep sleep. In the night I awoke to see Him step aside, but the power of His presence remained with me throughout the long night. I needed a man to stand in the gap for me. Someone to stand with me while I was alone and afraid, sick and in despair. I cried out to God—and He sent me Jesus.

Now, what is it that you need, friend? What is it that you need Him to do for you?

"The grave wrapped its ropes around me; death laid a trap in my path. But in my distress I cried out to the LORD; yes, I prayed to my God for help. He heard me from his sanctuary; my cry to him reached his ears" (Psalm 18:5–6 NLT).

Remembered by God

During my days in ICU, the Lord did something incredible for one of my nurses. I just happened to be in the right place at the right time for God to use me in the blessing.

I was probably her toughest patient to care for that evening. I had just come off the ventilator the day before and was still dealing with a lot of issues. Early evening after my family went home was a nightmare. I suddenly began coughing, gagging, choking, and throwing up all at the same time. I thought I might be having another near-death experience, but my nurse was quick and knew just what to do to help me. There we were in the middle of her schedule of passing out nighttime meds, and suddenly my nurse had a patient to clean up and a bed to change.

A couple of hours later, I was still coughing and gagging. To take my mind off my misery, I began praying for everyone who passed by my room, which was located right across from the nurses' station. It was unbelievable how busy they were in the middle of the night, but I found myself praying for emergency personnel as they wheeled in new patients, doctors, nurses, and family members who were brought in to see loved ones who were on the brink of death. My goodness, there were so many sick people, so many needs!

As I was praying, the Lord spoke in my spirit that I was to pray for the next person to enter my room. Not only was I to pray for that person, but I was to ask him or her if something was going on in their life that they needed prayer for. So I waited and waited, watching for the next person to enter my room.

When she walked in my room, I could tell that she was in a hurry, and she looked frustrated. She was my nurse, and I wondered if my perfect storm earlier in the evening had rattled her nerves and unraveled her schedule. But God was very specific that I was to ask the next person who entered how I could pray for him or her. So, as she filled my cup with ice and took care of other medical needs, I waited until she was fluffing my pillows and straightening my bed.

I said, "Thank you for helping me tonight. I appreciate your kindness. I wonder if there is something I can pray for you about, something that you need prayer for." She stopped what she was doing and looked at me. She said, "I don't understand. What did you say?" So, in my squeaky little voice, I repeated my question, asking if I could pray for her. Still looking puzzled, she replied, "You mean you'd like for me to pray for you?" And I said, "No. I just wondered if you had a need that I could pray for before I go to sleep tonight."

"What do you know? Who told you about me? Why would you ask me something like that?" She looked startled, and for a moment I thought she was offended and angry. I said, "Well, I've been praying all evening for everyone who passes by my door, and God spoke to my spirit, telling me I was to ask the next person who came in my room if there was something he or she needed prayer for. You are the first one to come in since He told me to do that, so I'm just asking what I can pray about for you as I get ready to sleep tonight."

Tears suddenly came flowing out of her eyes and down her cheeks. It took her a moment to recover, but she then said, "I'm a single mother, and my baby was born prematurely a few months ago. She is very sick tonight and in ICU in another town an hour away from here. She has a sickness much like yours. My mother is staying with her while I work. You could pray for that. Yes, you could pray for that."

I took her hand and said, "God wants you to know that He has not forgotten you. He is here with you while you work, and He is with your baby bringing healing to her body. While you are here taking such good care of me, He is with your mother and your baby taking good care of them."

We bowed our heads to pray. In the middle of my prayer, she stopped me to remind me my oxygen level was getting low, so I wrapped it up quickly and said, "Amen!" God is so good to me. I thank Him for using me in the middle of my personal nightmare to minister to someone whose need was far greater than mine. She walked out of my room thanking God for remembering her and wiping her eyes as she made her way to take care of another patient.

The Lord is so good, so kind. He heals the brokenhearted and binds up their wounds. He is merciful and gracious, sustaining us on our sickbeds, and He transforms a bed of death into health. Thank You, Lord! I will never forget what You've done for me. And, oh, gentle Yeshua. I will never forget what You did for my nurse.

"He healeth the broken in heart, and bindeth up their wounds" (Psalm 147:3).

"And ye shall serve the LORD your God, and he shall bless thy bread, and thy water; and I will take sickness away from the midst of thee" (Exodus 23:25).

Woodi's Arm

One of the most painful things I've ever experienced took place during a lengthy stay in ICU. If you've spent any time at all in there, you know I'm talking about the blood pressure cuff.

My left arm was very swollen and painful, with my fingers looking like swollen little sausages. The kids and Pat each took turns gently rubbing and healing me through their touch and love.

Every fifteen minutes the cuff automatically inflates and records the pressure. The thing is that it inflates fast and high causing enormous pain in the arm—it is explosive pain that lasts for approximately five minutes. It made me want to curse and swear. But it didn't seem quite right to curse that which was meant to bless and help the doctors save my life.

I'm not sure when it came about exactly. Possibly one or two days after the vent was removed. In the midst of tears, I called out to my husband to help me pray through the pain, through the tears, through the dark night of the soul that chases a person to the edge of despair.

"Please! Help me use this for good! Help me use this time to pray for our Woodi in Afghanistan."

I extended my arm the moment the machine turned on and the pumping sounded. (The first time I heard it following my vent removal, I was surprised to hear that it sounded like strange Asian music.) My beloved Pat was by my side gently holding my hand and supporting my arm. With broken vocal chords, I screeched out a prayer. "Oh, God! Father God! Our son Woodi needs you every minute. Please help Woodi to be strong and brave as he serves our family and our nation! Thank you for Woodi and Michele's great sacrifice during this sixth deployment! Surround the family with your protection from injury, harm, illness, or loss of life. Bless their children, Courtney, Colin, Hailey, and Ben. Thank you that Michele is faithfully leading the children to love Jesus. Whatever they need, Lord! Please provide for them while Woodi is away! You are their provider, their sustainer, their friend. Bless them with our love. They are warriors and need your strength! Please, give it to them all in double measure!"

The prayer never varied much. This excruciating time lovingly became known as "Woodi's Arm." And no matter the time, or whoever was in the room, we stopped to pray through the pain, the loss, and despair, and we gave it all back to God as praise for our good and His glory!

"For I reckon that the sufferings of this present time *are* not worthy *to be compared* with the glory which shall be revealed in us" (Romans 8:18).

"For our present troubles are small and won't last very long. Yet they produce for us a glory that vastly outweighs them and will last forever!" (2 Corinthians 4:17 NLT).

An Angel from the Lord

In early March 2016, something happened that almost took my life. I caught the flu. Oh, it wasn't just any flu—it was devil flu. It was type A influenza, which became a near-death illness for me as it progressed to double pneumonia, acute respiratory distress syndrome, and sepsis.

This illness was so severe that as I walked through the valley of the shadow of death, I was with Jesus. During that time, He did some pretty incredible things for me—miracles to return me back to my family alive. Every day we saw more and more of His healing hand upon me as I made progress in restoration of my health. It's been a long road back, but I gained little victories every day as God manifested His healing power in my body. With every breath I praised Him. Even in those long, sleepless nights, my screechy voice of thanksgiving was lifted up to Him.

One of the hardest things for me was a very harsh cough after I was removed from the vent. It sounded very wicked, not unlike a rabid dog barking. It was particularly bad during the eight days I was in the rehab unit at the hospital. I often coughed all night and day, getting no rest or relief. About two days before I was released from the hospital, I'd spent a grueling dark night of the soul with this cough. I put a little SOS out to my friends on social media asking for prayer. So many responded and lifted me up to the Lord throughout the night. I was grateful. Those prayers were a gift. They got me through.

Midmorning the next day, I had just returned from physical therapy and hoped to get some rest, but I was coughing, and coughing, and coughing. I just couldn't stop. Suddenly a beautiful, angel-like woman entered my room. Her golden hair was caught up in a ribbon. She wore a long white cloak with a white blouse and pants. She had a very distraught and concerned expression on her face.

As she entered, she said, "Oh, please! Tell me what is going on with you. You are clearly in distress and miserable. Tell me what has happened to you." In my scratchy, squeaky voice, I told her about my illness and my horrible cough that continued to plague me. She rose from her chair and walked to the door, exclaiming, "You need relief, and I am going to help you."

I had no idea who this angel was, only that God had sent her to me. Several minutes later I was sure of it as this beautiful angel gave my nurse some medicine for my cough. They were little golden pearls … surely they were heavenly pearls delivered personally by an angel from the Lord.

When my nurse helped me with the medicine, I asked about the beautiful woman. She said, "That was your doctor's assistant. She heard you coughing all the way down the hall and came to ask me about you. I told her to stand outside your door to listen for a moment, hoping that she could do something to help you. I've been so worried for you!"

I replied, "God sent her to me. She is a beautiful angel from the Lord, and she brought me these little golden pearls from heaven." We both smiled while I thanked Him for this precious gift.

God is so good to me, and He provided everything I needed during my illness. He is the strength of my life. I fear no evil because He is with me. He gives me comfort, and He continues to anoint my body with His healing. I continually give Him thanks and praise with every breath.

Prayers are a precious gift that I highly treasure. In His goodness and mercy, there were thousands of people all over the world lifting me up for His healing touch, begging God to save my life. He answered their prayers and even sent me angels and pearls from heaven to bring me comfort and rest. Thank you, my friends. I will never forget that you journeyed all the way to death's door and back with me.

> I love the LORD, because he hath heard my voice *and* my supplications. Because he hath inclined his ear unto me, therefore will I call upon *him* as long as I live. The sorrows of death compassed me, and the pains of hell gat hold upon me: I found trouble and sorrow. Then called I upon the name of the LORD; O LORD, I beseech thee, deliver my soul. Gracious *is* the LORD, and righteous; yea, our God *is* merciful. The LORD preserveth the simple: I was brought low, and he helped me. Return unto thy rest, O my soul; for the LORD hath dealt bountifully with thee. For thou hast delivered my soul from death, mine eyes from tears, *and* my feet from falling. I will walk before the LORD in the land of the living. (Psalm 116:1–9)

He Is the Strength of My Life

God continues to give me grace each day to see evidence of His healing hand in my life. As my breathing improves, I've begun moving around the house easier—doing a little laundry, picking up random items in the kitchen and living room and putting them where they belong. Today, I'm cleaning out some of the things we brought home from the hospital and straightening our bedroom.

When my family first told me that I was in the hospital because of illness, it was hard for me to believe. I have no memory of being sick, though I do have evidence such as text messages, medicines from the urgent care at Mercy, and the stories my family has shared with me. One of the things Pat told me was that my last day at home before being admitted to the hospital, it looked like I had crawled into my prayer closet to rest as there were a few books scattered about, a small blanket, and wadded-up Kleenexes. I haven't felt well enough to spend time in there this past month, but today I poked my head in and crawled up in the closet to put things away.

Some of my books were open, and it looked like I had tried to read as things were underlined … but I have no memory of having read what I underlined. I found the wadded-up Kleenex and cleared all of that away. But I also found something in my little photo album that I write scriptures in or doodles that I make on index cards while I study. I found a scripture that I had been meditating on the week before I got sick. It's the last one in the album, and I do remember writing it out and placing it between the clear pages. It is also an evidence of God working in my spirit, giving me what I needed even before I knew I needed it. It brings tears to my eyes knowing that God cares about me so much that He interacts in my life a number of ways. He does it to have a relationship with me, teach me, correct me, encourage and inspire me.

He gave me this Word to prepare me for this great trial, this walk through the valley of the shadow of death—my dark night of the soul. Here is His Word, the last Word I received from Him before I became ill: "My health may fail and my spirit may grow weak, but God remains the strength of my heart. He is mine forever" (Psalm 73:26 NLT).

Friends, if He loves me that much, the Word tells us that He loves you that much too! Draw close to Him, and He will draw close to you. He will tell you great and mighty things that you do not know. He will give you everything you need for life and godliness. He will shower you with His mercy, His grace, His strength, His wisdom, and yes, even His healing power.

Lord, thank You for Your blessing on my life. Thank You for walking with me in the valley and for being my hope, my life, and my strength. Thank You for this evidence that You will prepare me for what lies ahead if I will just seek You and spend time with You. You are indeed the strength of my heart. You are mine forever, and I am Yours.

A True Miracle

I recently had an appointment with a doctor I hadn't seen for about eight months. I typically see her yearly, but because of a near-death illness, I was required to follow up with her after extensive rehab before I returned to work. When she heard I was coming in early for my appointment, she read my patient folder from the previous three months. The first thing she said to me as she entered the examining room was, "I can't even believe you are here! Do you know what a miracle it is that you didn't die?"

This doctor has twenty years of experience in pulmonary medicine. As I related to her what I'd personally been through the past few months, she had tears in her eyes. She was shocked that I had lived to tell about it. As we finished up the exam and follow-up paperwork, she said, "This is a miracle. A true miracle. You just made my day! This is the best story I've had in months." She briefly hugged me and whispered, "I'm so glad you made it."

I pray that I don't ever forget what a miracle it is that I'm still here. That I'm alive is a miracle! I'm still with my family and all of you that I hold so dear. I still have things to do. With every sunrise, I add to the number of my days. Thank you, Lord, for blessing me with life, love, and work to do for the kingdom.

If you are still here, alive in this world, your life is a miracle too! Life is such a gift, and even in the worst of circumstances, we can trust Him with our futures.

"'For I know the plans I have for you,' says the LORD. 'They are plans for good and not for disaster, to give you a future and a hope'" (Jeremiah 29:11 NLT).

He is our hope, friend! He is the strength of our lives, and He has prepared for us a wonder-filled future with Him if we will receive the Lord Jesus Christ. Believe and receive. You will have comfort in every sorrow, strength for every weakness, joy for every despairing day, and hope for every dark night of the soul.

I know this to be true. You do not walk alone through the valley of the shadow of death. He is with you then, and through His Holy Spirit, He is with you now.

He is Emmanuel, God with us. And He is the Holy Spirit of the living God, God in us. With us and in us. What a miracle! What a gift! Thank you, Father!

"Every good gift and every perfect gift is from above, and cometh down from the Father of lights, with whom is no variableness, neither shadow of turning" (James 1:17).

It's Supernatural

When I say I have hair angst, some of you know exactly what I'm talking about. My hair has been the cause of much fretting and stewing from the very beginning of my days. It started with a pixie cut gone awry when I was just one or two years old and continued through numerous home perms inflicted by my mother, who loved to put a little curl in my impossibly straight hair.

The early 1970s were my best hair days. Straight as a string was the fashion—I didn't have to do a thing.

In recent years, I've bemoaned going from red hair to gray, finally giving in to wear the color God gave me. For years it's been a forty-five-minute chore raking through my bedhead, using a large curling iron for body, my favorite brush for ratting, and a can of hair spray to hold it all in place. The chore has become even more burdensome since my near-death illness.

I was in such despair when following my illness my hair started falling out by the handfuls. It's very common following a traumatic illness, but the amount of hair in the bottom of the sink and tub left me horrified. It wasn't unusual for it to cling to my sweater or float to ground.

I spent many nights searching through pages and pages of wigs, wondering which one would become mine. The relief I felt eight months later when my hair sprouted new growth was enormous. But imagine my shock when it came back in curls! Lots and lots of little loose curls.

I've been fighting with it for a few months now, not really sure what to do with it. The ritual of raking, smoothing, ratting, and spraying takes forever, and the results haven't been that great. Much to my horror, it began to take on a life of its own.

About a month ago I somehow injured my shoulder, and unable to raise my arm high enough to smooth the curls out with a straightening iron and rat it up to a proper height, I had to show up at work with my Saturday hair—hair that hangs in little ringlets. Believe me—that was as painful as my shoulder. I've complained about it incessantly, much to the ire of everyone who lives with me. Poor Pat.

One morning I had an epiphany of sorts. Only someone with such quirkiness and hair angst could have an epiphany about newly acquired curly hair, but that I did.

A few days post vent during my illness, I thanked God for His healing mercies, but I asked Him to leave me a mark. Oh, I didn't want to be disabled, I just wanted a mark to always remind me of the miracle God did for me. For almost a year, I thought the mark was a bruise on my arm from the pic line where they gave me drugs. In recent days that mark has begun to fade, and now I can barely see it. I lamented that fact one morning as I was grieving over wearing my curly Saturday hair to work.

As I fretted over my curly head, a quiet voice spoke in my heart, "What if this is your mark?"

What? What did you say?

"Qené, this is it. This is your mark."

Now, it's taken me awhile to quiet my complaints, but I am learning that if God has chosen to answer my prayer, even in a very unexpected way, then it is disobedience not to receive it. I certainly am more peaceful just resting in what the Lord has provided in a miraculous way.

So, while I enjoy the extra time I now have in the mornings, and while my shoulder continues to mend, and while my Pat laughs at his curly-headed Q. tagging along to work everyday, God has given me a reminder, a very visible testimony, that there are miracles to be found in Him. Ah, yes! My God rejoices over me with singing and with—curls.

He's done a miracle in me! I am alive. I am His. He is mine. And He will never, ever leave me nor forsake me. He even helps me curl my hair. How precious Yeshua, my Lord, is to me.

When people ask me if my hair is naturally curly, I now respond, "No, my hair is supernaturally curly."

Benediction—How Shall We Then Walk?

———

I remember what fun we had teaching our children to walk. It didn't take long to discover there is a reason that we call them toddlers. First-born, P. J. started toddling the week of his first birthday—one month before Woodi was born. Once he got started, he never stopped, and he often ran circles around his tired mommy. He'd often race through the house as fast as he could, come to a screeching halt, sound effects included, and race back to give me a kiss. Oh, I could live in that memory for a while!

Our funny Woodi didn't want to walk at all. He had mastered the art of rolling. He rolled all through the house, so there was no need for him to walk. He was fast and so very funny. He learned to say his own name before ever saying the usual "mumma" and "dada." He entertained us for hours rolling through the house, loudly proclaiming, "Woooodeee. Woooodeee." What a joy that memory is to me!

Our Noni was a late walker. She loved crawling, though it was painful to watch. Oh, my! She crawled with her right hand turned upside down, on her wrist. In fact, she even wore a callus on the top of her little hand. She was talking in sentences long before she walked! She was fifteen months old when she finally took off in consecutive steps, erasing all worries about having to piggy-back her down the wedding aisle!

One week after my near-death illness, I toddled along the length of my body while my physical therapist, "Marvelous Marvin," held on to me with a belt. That five feet, two inches felt like a mile. It was impressive enough that my Pat and Marvin applauded my effort! I said, "Thank you very much, Marvelous Marvin!" He quickly replied, "You are so welcome Queenly Qene'!"

Actually, I've been putting one foot in front of the other for a lot of years now, but as a believer in Christ, I am still learning how to walk with Him. Many years ago, all of twenty or more, the Lord taught me how He wants me to walk with Him. I'm a slow learner, but it is the desire of my heart to follow in His footsteps each day! How shall we then walk?

- In the light of His love! "But if we walk in the light, as he is in the light, we have fellowship one with another, and the blood of Jesus Christ his Son cleanseth us from all sin" (1 John 1:7).

- In the truth of His Word! "Sanctify them through thy truth: thy word is truth" (John 17:17).

- In the strength of His Spirit! "That he would grant you, according to the riches of his glory, to be strengthened with might by his Spirit in the inner man" (Ephesians 3:16–19).

- In the hope of His promises! "Blessed is the man that trusteth in the Lord, and whose hope the Lord is. For he shall be as a tree planted by the waters, and that spreadeth out her roots by the river, and shall not see when heat cometh, but her leaf shall be green; and shall not be careful in the year of drought, neither shall cease from yielding fruit" (Jeremiah 17:7–8).

I love walking with Christ—and I love walking with you! Thank you for the blessing you are to me. I pray you have enjoyed our little journey of walking through my stories and the Word of God. Many blessings to you, my beloved friend, as you learn to walk with our Yeshua in a peace unfettered by fear, stress, and anxieties of the world! Shalom!

"May the LORD bless thee, and keep thee: The LORD make his face shine upon thee, and be gracious unto thee: The LORD lift up his countenance upon thee, and give thee peace" (Numbers 6:24–26).

Questions for Further Personal or Group Study

After each story or prayer ask:

1. How did this story or prayer make you feel?
2. Have you ever encountered a similar circumstance or prayed a similar prayer?
3. Does this story leave you encouraged, or is there some action you feel led to take?
4. Will reading this help anyone you know? Perhaps there is someone you need to pray for?
5. Can you identify scriptures Qené used within the body of her story or prayer?
6. What other scriptures does this story or prayer bring to mind?
7. Take a few minutes to write your own story or your own prayer.
8. Ask God to help you give voice to what He is speaking to you, either on paper or through a testimony, one-on-one or in a group setting.
9. At the end of each story or prayer, take note of one or two verses that you would like to commit to memory.

When I first began following hard after Christ, I couldn't get enough of His Word. After years of never reading the scriptures, I suddenly found myself with a voracious appetite for it. I often went on a reading binge filled with wonder that the Holy Spirit opened my eyes to see the truth of it. There were so many things I didn't know! It's become my habit over the years to memorize and pray scriptures—using them in conversation or in my writings. The Word is so hidden in my heart that it naturally flows from my mouth and my pen. It could be that you will recognize them as you read them in my stories and prayers. As you identify them, I pray you will use that as an opportunity to dig a little deeper into the Word.

Notes

(Endnotes)

1   Robert Robinson, "Come Thou Fount of Every Blessing," Public Domain, https://us.search.ccli.com/songs/3015616/come-thou-fount-of-every-blessing

2   Catholic Answers, The Immaculate Conception and Assumption of Mary, https://www.catholic.com/tract/immaculate-conception-and-assumption

3   Catholic Doors, Frequently Asked Questions Regarding The Banns of Marriage, http://catholicdoors.com/faq/qu708.htm

4   Catholic Answers, Mixed Marriage, Jim Blackburn, August 4,2011, https://www.catholic.com/qa/in-a-mixed-marriage-does-the-couple-have-to-promise-to-raise-their-children-catholic-to-be

5   Cristendom-Awake Website, Praying with Non-Catholics—Is it Possible? Fr. Thomas Crean O.P., Feb 8, 2009 http://christendom-awake.org/pages/thomas-crean/praying-with-non-catholics.htm

6   Merriam-Webster, Definition of the word *hide*, https://www.merriam-webster.com/dictionary/hide

7   Hoffman, Elisha Albright; and Wilbanks, Keith, "Are You Washed in the Blood", Public Domain, https://us.search.ccli.com/songs/5713899/are-you-washed-in-the-blood

8   Jensen, Gordon, "Bigger Than Any Mountain", fair use, https://us.search.ccli.com/songs/56541/bigger-than-any-mountain?fromSearch=true

9   Billy Graham Evangelistic Association, Graham, Billy, My Heart Aches for America, July 19, 2012, https://billygraham.org/story/billy-graham-my-heart-aches-for-america/

10 The Phrase Finder, Gary Martin, Careless Talk Costs Lives – Loose Lips Sink Ships; https://www.phrases.org.uk/meanings/237250.html

11 Newton, John, (1725–1807); "Amazing Grace" public domain

12 Lennon, John; McCartney, Paul 1962 "Do You Want to Know a Secret?"

13 Difference Between.com, Admin 11-06-2014, http://www.differencebetween.com/difference-between-perception-and-vs-perspective/

About the Author

Qené Jeffers is an administrative assistant in a national ministry which facilitates missionaries serving in the United States. She is a mom to three and NéNé to ten. She loves rainy days, flea-marketing, and piddling around the house in her jammies. Qené lives in southwest Missouri with her husband Pat, where they serve in rural churches and raise backyard chickens.

Qené is available to teach Bible study and speak at women's ministry events. You may connect with her online at www.qenemanonjeffers.com or https://qsqueue.wordpress.com/

In Memory of Our Mother
Jené Gray Sharp
December 28, 1932 ~ December 14, 2013
Grove, Oklahoma

Who would have thought that we could live without you
for even one day? Or that we would feel such sorrow when
the angels welcomed you home and the radio played the
"Hallelujah Chorus" with your last earthly breath? Rest well,
beloved Momma. We will see you again – when it's time.

My birth forever changed your life, and your death forever changed mine.

In Memory of Our Sister
Patricia "Tish" Konen Rockwood
March 18, 1956 ~ December 29, 2017
Kamuela, Hawaii

Tish! Your sudden departure has left us stunned and brokenhearted
over our loss of you. How will we ever forgive that cat?

Twenty-two thousand, five hundred, and sixty-six sunsets
just weren't enough. We'll cross a river of memories and
cling to all our favorites remembering you. Enjoy the real
paradise as you wait for us there with Mother and Daddy,
and all the rest. Until then, we'll miss you, T-Boo.

And then there were five ~ René, Qené, Jay, Canera and Marni

You are both loved with an everlasting love –
My first thought in the morning, and my last prayer at night.
Jesus, Momma. Jesus, Tish.

Edwards Brothers Inc.
Ann Arbor MI. USA
April 13, 2018